THE PRESENCE OF
M·Y·T·H

THE PRESENCE OF
M·Y·T·H

Leszek Kolakowski

Translated by
Adam Czerniawski

The University of Chicago Press
CHICAGO AND LONDON

LESZEK KOLAKOWSKI is professor in the Committee on
Social Thought and the Department of Philosophy at the University
of Chicago and a fellow of All Souls College, Oxford University.
The author of some twenty-five books, he is perhaps best known for
his monumental three-volume *Mainstreams of Marxism*. Among his
many honors, Professor Kolakowski was the 1986 Jefferson
Lecturer, the highest honor conferred by the U. S. government for
outstanding achievement in the humanities.

First published in France in 1972 as *Obecność mitu* (Issue 224
in the *Biblioteka Kultury*) by the Institut Litteraire, Paris.
© 1972 by Leszek Kolakowski. A German translation was
published in 1973: © R. Piper & Co. Verlag, München 1973.

The University of Chicago Press, Chicago 60637
The University of Chicago Press, Ltd., London
© 1989 by The University of Chicago
All rights reserved. Published 1989
Printed in the United States of America

98 97 96 95 94 93 92 91 90 89   54321

LIBRARY OF CONGRESS CATALOGING-IN-PUBLICATION DATA

Kołakowski, Leszek.
  [Obecność mitu. English]
  The presence of myth / Leszek Kolakowski: translated by
Adam Czerniawski.
    p. cm.
  "First published in France in 1972 as Obecność mitu
(Issue 224 in the Biblioteka Kultury) by the Institut
Litteraire, Paris"—T.p. verso.
  Includes index.
  ISBN 0-226-45041-4
  1. Myth. 2. Culture. 3. Man. I. Title.
B4691.K586303413 1989
128—dc19   88-37054
                                             CIP

CONTENTS

PREFACE TO THE ENGLISH EDITION

This is a very, very old book. It was written in Polish in 1966; but the censoring authorities, despite the lengthy efforts of the publishing house, forbade its publication in Poland. It was eventually published in Polish in France in 1972 by Institut Littéraire, and in German translation by Piper Verlag. When I was reading it after so many years, it struck me how strongly my philosophical language was then dependent on German and French (mainly German) phenomenological and existential idiom, and to what extent this influence contributed to a stylistic heaviness which was probably avoidable. This was the reason why it could be translated relatively smoothly into German (according to my experience Polish and German are virtually the same language if we leave aside vocabulary, grammar, syntax, and phonetics); whereas to render it in English turned out to be an extremely arduous task in which, in spite of the hard and skillful work of my friend Adam Czerniawski, some clumsiness could not be avoided. If I had been compelled to write it in English, I would have probably expressed the same idea in another text. Too late.

Chicago, 20 July 1988

PREFACE

This little book is a concise summary of a nonexistent treatise, which its potential readers will in all probability be spared. I wanted it to be brief and, therefore, as far as possible, devoid of examples, historical anecdotes, footnotes, names, quotations, extensive classifications, digressions, reservations, and polemics. The price of the virtue of brevity are the vices of a certain dryness, monotony, and inadequate documentation. Nor is it a learned treatise (particularly in the realms of religious studies, mythography, sociology, or the psychology of myth), but an attempt to present a certain point of view with regard to a sensitive problem constantly present in the philosophy of culture. This problem concerns the localization in culture of mythopoeic production in relation to the structural characteristics of human consciousness.

The term "myth," whose precise definition I do not attempt and whose meaning, so I assume, emerges from the discourse as a whole, requires a certain initial stipulation. Its range overlaps the range demarcated by the study of religion. It covers a group—essential, it is true, but numerically insignificant—of religious myths, that is, the myths of Beginning. It also includes certain constructions, present (be they hidden or explicit) in our intellectual and affective life, namely, those which conditioned and mutable elements of experience allow us to bind teleologically by appeal to unconditioned realities (such as "being," "truth," and "value"). I attempt to justify this identification through a basic identity of functions which these various products of human spiritual life perform. I also attempt to explain how the inevitability of these functions in cultural life can be explained, and also in what sense they are not capable of coexistence with its technological and scientific efforts.

The mythological character of these derivative constructs constitutes the guiding notion of this discourse. Their parity with myth in the primary sense of the word comes about as a result of one particularly significant function. I do not therefore take into account those qualities of myth—especially their narrative qualities—which validate a search for their extensions in works of artistic imagination.

Such a generalized employment of a word which already has its rules of application more or less fixed may be open to criticism. But I could find no other which would better designate the realm I am concerned with. Relying on the authority of A. N. Whitehead, I may add that the whole of philosophical endeavor depends on attempts at constructing concepts which are more and more general, for whose designation the existing vocabulary is never sufficiently rich. If one prefers to avoid arbitrary coinage, one has therefore to make use of words which lie closest to the projected realm and to give them an extended meaning. In philosophical reflection inherited words usually appear incompetent through excessive usage, while rashly constructed neologisms quickly turn into insufferable oddities, as numerous examples demonstrate. It is therefore safer to try out the possibilities embedded in existing terminology, taking care not to be carried away without resistance by its inertia and maintaining an alertness to meanings which are smuggled even subconsciously into the classification of the world in colloquial speech. All attempts at exposing hidden implications of language may be useful.

I attempt to employ the generalized concept of myth as a net to catch a permanently constitutive element of culture, and thus to create a somewhat different principle of classifying phenomena than is most often accepted in the philosophy of culture. I am convinced that the crucial boundary between the mythological layer of culture and its technological and scientific layer runs differently from what might be judged on the basis of most generally known functional interpretations of man's mythological creativity. The "differently" is not, however, simply the outcome of a different meaning arbitrarily assigned to the term "myth." On the contrary, that altered sense arises from the conviction that religious mythologies are a certain variant or a historical particularization of a phenomenon which may be grasped in a more fundamental characterization; and that the essential functional bond links these mythologies with products found in all human intercourse (and in our civilization as well); in intellectual activities, in artistic creativity, in language, in coexistence covered by moral values, in technological endeavors, and in sexual life. I am, therefore, attempting to trace the presence of myth in non-mythical areas of experience and thought. Thus, for example, I do not think one should draw on the opposition of the two hetero-genous blocks, science and religion. And not only because religious phenomena function as tools in various spheres of com-munal life, but also because the basic validations of the scientific efforts make use of the labors of mythical consciousness. For similar reasons I attempt, as far as possible, to free myself from such oppositions as intellect/intuition, thought/emotion, and others.

Further, I attempt to embrace the category so constructed also in its functional and genetic identity, referring its variants to a common source, that is, to certain irremovable attributes of the existential constitution of consciousness and its references to the world of nature. I have tried to describe the character of a need which gives birth to the constantly renewed interpretations of the empirical world as a place of exile or a step on the way back to unconditioned Being. In this sense—if such remarks can avoid pretentiousness—these are footnotes to the most classical texts of our culture: Book 7 of Plato's *Republic*, the third chapter of Gene-sis and the second dialogue of the *Bhagavad Gita*.

The extent to which my thought in these matters owes a debt to other philosophers, whose work is known to me in varying degrees, I attempt occasionally to indicate, probably without suf-ficient scrupulousness; but I am convinced that in many instances this is self-evident to a reader with professional knowledge in this field—and is not, in any event, very important. I venture to say—and in this I merely follow many brave masters of the art of philosophy—that I am simply making available the existing in-heritance. This enables me to refrain from a precise division between thoughts that are mine and those that are others', es-pecially since this is an impossible task; for it is impossible to remember all those to whom one owes something, and in the final analysis it would assuredly turn out that whatever we have, we owe to others.

Although the whole of this discourse consists of scraps of thoughts collected during various historical researches, it carries a certain significance for me. I well understand that from this it does not follow that it should carry any weight with others. It seems to me, however, that attempts to return to fundamental questions, if they are connected with a reasonably unprejudiced effort of the imagination, cannot be completely empty even though they never achieve complete success. The construction of new linguistic tools to express always the same questions is the fate of the philosophical endeavor. One may regard this fate as proof of the hopelessness of the effort as such, but one may also see in it an argument for the liveliness of the inquiring position. It is a natural phenomenon that in the first moments of the awakening of independent reflection we pose the questions that we then repeat in our final thoughts. It is puzzling that we do not command a spiritual energy that would satisfy our curiosity, but it is even more puzzling that knowing this, we still have enough energy to keep on asking the questions. "Less than All cannot satisfy Man" (Blake).

Warsaw, November 1966

1

PRELIMINARY DISTINCTIONS

1

The labor of the analytical mind which produces science is the organ in human culture which tames the physical environment. Science is the extension of civilization's technological core. In the scientific sense, "true" means that which has the chance of being employed in effective technological procedures. This is not to say that the criteria we employ in settling scientific questions always depend on the likely possibilities of a practical application of the acquired solution. In their general shape, however, these criteria are so constructed that they enable us to reject from the area of valid knowledge whatever has no chance of technological application. Popular thought and scientific thought, as well as language, are correlated, in the overriding evolutionary strategy, with the physical survival of the species.

2

Metaphysical questions and beliefs are technologically barren and are therefore neither part of the analytical effort nor an element of science. As an organ of culture they are an extension of the mythical core. They are concerned with the absolutely primal conditions of the realm of experience; they concern the quality of Being as a whole (as distinct from the object); they concern the necessity of events. They aim at revealing the relativity of the world of experience and attempt to reveal an unconditioned reality, thanks to which the conditioned reality becomes intelligible.

3

Metaphysical questions and beliefs reveal an aspect of human existence not revealed by scientific questions and beliefs, namely, that aspect that refers intentionally to nonempirical unconditioned reality. The presence of this intention does not guarantee the existence of the referents. It is only evidence of a need, alive in culture, that that to which the intention refers should be present. But this presence cannot in principle be the object of proof, because the proof-making ability is itself a power of the analytical mind, technologically oriented, which does not extend beyond its tasks. The idea of proof, introduced into metaphysics, arises from a confusion of two different sources of energy active in man's conscious relation to the world: the technological and the mythical.

4

Let us attempt a description of the need which generates answers to questions that are ultimate and metaphysical—that is, incapable of conversion into scientific questions. Before considering the sources of this need in inadequately conceived and unclear conditions connected with the permanent situation of human consciousness as such in the world, let us consider the circumstances of which people are generally aware and which are visible on the surface of culture. At this level, this need can be described in at least three ways. First, as a need to make the empirical realities understandable; that is, to grasp the world of experience as intelligible by relating it to the unconditioned reality which binds phenomena teleologically. The purposeful order of the world cannot be deduced from what may validly be regarded as the experimental material of scientific thought; it cannot therefore form a valid hypothesis to explain the data of experience. An affirmation of this order represents an understanding interpretation of these data. The point of view that denies the right to such an interpretation may signify either a refusal to accept ultimate questions—that is, it may be a paralysis or a dulling of that aspect of human existence which is intentionally directed to transcendence—or it may be a conscious acceptance of the world's absurdity. A language which attempts to reach transcendence directly violates, to no purpose, its own technological instrumentality. It reaches transcendence in myths which give a meaning to empirical realities and practical activities via relativization. A mythical organization of the world (that is, the rules of understanding empirical realities as meaningful) is permanently present in culture. The objection that such an organization does not become true as a result of its permanence, or of the reality of the needs which give rise to it, has no argumentative power for a consciousness whose mythopoeic stratum has been aroused, since here the predicates "true" and "false" are inapplicable. Here it is not the case of matching a judgment with a situation it describes but of matching a need with an area which satisfies it. Myth degenerated when it changed into a doctrine, that is, a product demanding and seeking proof. Attempts at imitating knowledge are the form which brings about the degeneration of faith. The experience of correlating a need with that area of Being which satisfies it cannot be questioned as invalid from the point of view of scientific knowledge, so long as this experience is differentiated from the justificatory procedures.

5

Another version of this need for answers to ultimate questions is the need for faith in the permanence of human values. Human values become personalized the moment natural evolution reaches the point of personal existence. Where the disappearance of personality is total, the values tied to personal existence are strictly confined to that existence, while if they are inherited in a material, objective manner by continuous human groups, they enjoy a second parallel existence while these groups last. The totality of values produced by individuals, that is, the totality of values called into existence by human beings, does therefore tend towards their ultimate disappearance. In other words, our efforts, even when extended in their material results beyond the existence of individuals, are totally dissolved in the disintegration of physical existence, since neither humanity nor the earth is eternal. Thus, the belief in personal survival is not a postulate, since it can have no conceivable justification; it is a way of affirming personal values. Such an affirmation has the same kind of validity in culture as do other mythopoeic acts, so long as they are the product of a real need.

6

A third version of the same need is the desire to see the world as continuous. The world undergoes change by mutations and reveals discontinuities at critical points. From an empirical knowledge of the properties of the elements we are unable at critical points to educe the properties of the complexes: we have to establish independently that under certain conditions properties of elements reveal new properties of complexes. We do not know in what way the properties of the organic world are included in the construction of inanimate matter, in what manner the properties of human intelligence are included in the attributes of life. We guess at discontinuities, that is, we speculate that transitions *need not have occurred* on the basis of the properties themselves of a previous state. (The laws which state that under specified conditions specified phenomena always occur describe what in fact occurs; they include no indication that this *must* occur; they may, it is true, be explained as more precise versions of more general regularities, but these more general regularities never as a rule—and not just occasionally—cross the barrier of facticity of "contingency" in the Leibnizian sense of the word.) We therefore wish to comprehend the mutation as an act of choice which establishes continuity. A transcendence capable of choice satisfies the need to see the world as continuous. The presence of transcendence does not therefore become a hypothesis, since scientific thought does not establish any necessities for continuities. Thus, the desire for continuity is not a reason which transforms myth into a thesis—it motivates conviction.

7

In enumerating the three forms in which the need for myth appears on the surface of our culture, I treated them as three versions or variants of the same phenomenon. It does seem in fact that the same common motivation appears in all of them: the desire to arrest physical time by imposing upon it a mythical form of time; that is, one which allows us to see in the mutability of things not only *change,* but also *accumulation,* or allows us to believe that what is past is retained—as far as values are concerned—in what endures; that facts are not merely facts, but are building blocks of a universe of values which it is possible to salvage despite the irreversible flow of events. A belief in a purposeful order, hidden in the stream of experience, allows us to judge that in what passes there grows and is preserved something which does not pass away; that in the impermanence of events there is a growth of significance which is not directly perceived; that therefore decomposition and destruction affect only the visible layer of existence, without touching the other, which is resistant to decay. This same conquest of temporality is achieved in myths, which make possible a belief in the permanence of personal values. Here also mutability and annihilation may be regarded as the fate of the phenomenal layer of humanity; but seen from a mythical perspective, they themselves become stages in the growth of values. Similarly, belief in the continuity of changes, where apparent mutational leaps are the work of choice, is merely the necessary completion of an order, where what is past and is passing is capable of survival as far as its nonempirical normative layer is concerned and —with reference to a nontemporal order—can resist time.

Thus, even a most cursory glance shows us that in all instances we are concerned with the same problem: to avoid acceptance of a contingent world which expends itself on each occasion in its impermanent state, which is what it is now and bears no reference to anything else.

Only at this point, which we note as almost obvious, there appears the proper question regarding the sources of this desire which is supposed to reveal to us the location of the world in a nontemporal construct. For the appearance of this desire is not in itself intelligible and demands clarification in the very conditions which make culture possible.

8

Thus, all reasons in which the mythical consciousness is rooted, both in its initial variant, and in its metaphysical extensions, are acts affirming values. They can be fruitful to the extent that they satisfy the real need for controlling the world of experience by a meaning-giving interpretation of it, referring it to unconditioned Being. But the ultimate reasons which guide the choice of what is asserted in scientific thought are also acts of evaluation. In acknowledging the value of increased energies, which the human group can command in exploiting the physical environment, we create the necessary condition for the criteria of choice between truth and falsehood. These criteria are not in a historical sense arbitrary, that is, their coming about and triumph can be historically explained. They are, however, arbitrary in the logical sense, that is, there are no rules of logic which precede these criteria and enable us to justify them. On the contrary, the rules of logic are the product of the presence of these criteria.

9

That is why the opposition between a meaning-generating faith and an explanatory science has a somewhat different sense than is generally considered by positivists. Both have their own reasons embedded in cultural values; neither is rooted in transcendental norms of cognitions, because such norms, if they exist, cannot be known by us. The values on which each flourishes are different. We shall have to reflect upon the sense in which their irreconcilability is accidental (that is, defined in civilizational terms) and the sense in which it appears irreversible. But undoubtedly it is possible to remove the logical form of collision if we do not attempt to fix the value of myth as technologically (that is, scientifically) valuable. However, a faulty differentiation between the mythical, the ritualistic, and the technological functions performed by various elements of communal life is all too common. Undoubtedly, certain activities and products of culture perform a dual or a triple function, particularly if they have a common root—for instance, certain areas of art. This makes confusion in interpretation more likely, but it does not make differentiation impossible. Stagnant societies drew technical activities into a ritualistic and mythical order, so that they had their sacred aspects and took place within a wider order, which gave sense to them; nevertheless—as Malinowski observes—the differentiation between effectiveness arising from a sacred order and technical effectiveness is clear in these societies. Technologically orientated culture has taken up a contrary effort: It wishes to include myth in the technological order, that is, to turn myth into an element of cognition in the same sense in which science is cognition—it seeks justification for myth. This grotesque effort at rationalization has created caricatures of myth which have affected the Christian religion in particular. Attempts to arrest this decadence. which was for long perceived as a sign of progress, are now being undertaken. These are attempts to reestablish myth in its primal dignity. There is no certainty they will succeed.

10

Myth cannot be reached by persuasion; persuasion belongs to a different area of interpersonal communication, that is, to an area in which the criteria of technological resilience of judgments have their force. From time to time discursive philosophy has contributed to a flowering of mythical consciousness, even though it was unable in a valid manner to press the content of myths into the resources of analytical reason, where in general it is able to survive only thanks to its own passivity—inert and barren, like empty book jackets on library shelves. So, first, philosophy may awaken self-knowledge regarding the significance that ultimate questions carry in human life. Second, it can in the light of these questions reveal the absurdity of regarding a relative world as a self-sufficient reality. Third, it can open up the possibility of interpreting the world of experience as a conditioned world. It can do no more. The passing of this possibility into actuality is the achievement of personal consciousness, initiating a spontaneous movement of understanding at the moment when a dormant particle intentionally targeted at mythical reality comes to life in it. This motion is neither proof nor ratiocination. It is the awakening of mythical consciousness.

11

The sense of continuity in relation to tradition may, but need not, help mythical consciousness. There is always a reason which needs to be revealed in the permanence of myths and the inertia of conservatism. Values are transmitted only through social inheritance, that is, thanks to a radiation of authoritative tradition. The inheritance of myths is the inheritance of values which myths impose. Thus, coherence of human coexistence demands that tradition as such—and not just because in the past it had been judged a good tradition—should radiate authority. But from this

it does not yet follow that the values of myth are wholly imma-
nent in relation to these values which myth transmits and which
human societies require. Nor does it follow that one ought to
worship tradition unreservedly. Particular traditions stay alive or
lose their force and wither, depending on a variety of conditions;
they live and die like human beings. Jung and Eliade have attempted to demonstrate that individual myths are locally and
historically determined particularizations of that myth which
makes up the common archetypal pool of mythical consciousness,
although it manifests itself only in culturally designated specifics.
These attempts themselves appear to form part of mythopoeic
endeavors, and it is difficult to imagine how one could endow
them with the status of a hypothesis. They are perhaps worthy of
our attention as ecumenical efforts, that is, as elements of an
endeavor which remains within mythical consciousness; but, it
seems, they are unlikely to succeed as an effort which attempts to
make mythical consciousness the object of scientific reflection
only.

2

MYTH WITHIN THE EPISTEMOLOGICAL INQUIRY

1

What were philosophers after when they inquired whether an object is *outside* or *beyond* an act of perception? The term "beyond" and similar ones characterize a purely topological relationship, or, in a wider sense, the negation of any relationship of belonging of an element to its class. The topological sense suggests itself most readily, but it is equally easy to reveal the absurdity of its application in such an inquiry. For it would mean that we know what space is and are consequently asking whether an object spatially defined is situated in a place where the perceiving ego—also defined spatially—is not. No philosopher who has understood the question in this way has ever replied that the object is a spatial part of the perceiving body, since space itself appears in so-called subjectivist doctrines as derivative from the act of perception.

If the word "beyond" indicates that the element does not belong to a class, what is the class in question? A class of the so-called acts of experience? But we do not know the meaning of the claim that a perceived object is not an element of the act of perception as a whole. (The distinction—in Meinong and Twardowski—between the act, the content, and the object of perception is a derivative abstraction, implying a realist metaphysic, and cannot therefore appear in the assumptions of the inquiry into the validity of that metaphysic.) But, they would say, the question is whether it exists in reality, whether there is an object present in a situation in which an act of perception does not occur. We do not, however, possess any obvious intuition of existence other than that of belonging to a particular class. So the question would be: does the object belong to a class of objects

9

irrespective of the perceptual situation? In order to answer it we would have to have at our disposal an intuition of presence (of existence) of that class of objects which would itself be capable of description in relation to that class of which it would be a subclass, that is, finally, in relation to the most general class—the universe or everything. But the question, Does everything exist? cannot be meaningfully put precisely because we lack an intuition of absolute existence (that is, of existence other than that of belonging to a class). The question is based on a false assumption and cannot therefore be formulated.

But the question has also been put differently. The act of perception is *mine,* so that if an object is identical with a certain property of an act (its content), the object is *my* attribute, that is, an attribute of the so-called ego self-experiencing its own identity. However, the Cartesian illusion embedded in this question (that is, the illusion that we experience an inescapable intuition of the ego) has been effectively revealed by, for instance, Husserl and William James as an abstraction imported into experience. There is no ego in perception.

2

If, however, following Avenarius and James, we accept experience as primal material, indivisible into various substrates such as body and consciousness, the question arises whether we have solved the problem of the so-called existential independence of objects, or whether we have rejected it as faultily presented. It seems that the latter is the case, for it is true that we do not experience an object and the awareness of an object separately; that is Avenarius's thesis, but already present in another formulation in the doctrine of St. Augustine. One can reasonably hold that this distinction arises from a prejudice implanted into Aristotelian categories. But persisting prejudices always require consideration, the more so when, thanks to their insistence, they have created a situation in which experience, as the primal material, does not appear intuitively more accessible than the just abolished elements in the dichotomy of body and mind. The source of the prejudice lies in the need to experience human community. The community may be constituted by an object, that is, by our presence within something which is self-identical in relation to every perceiver. By the same token, every perceiver must be defined as one of the objects, since only in relation to an object can the perceiver be grasped; but perception has to distinguish the human object, hence the separate names to characterize its substrate nature: soul, subject, consciousness, and mind.

Perhaps that culture, in which the sense of a community was dominated by a shared resistance towards nature perceived as raw and unpolished, had in a natural way shaped the concept of substance and gave birth to the epistemological inquiry. It may be that a culture, in which dependence is experienced in relation to a culturally organized world, in relation to human products, does not need to constitute the sense of community around the distinction between subject and object, but is capable of recognizing the primacy of the act of perception in relation to that distinction. Since the beginning of the nineteenth century, new versions of the anthropocentric perspective have grown. These versions reject Berkeley's question, because they reject the distinction between subject and object, both in the Cartesian version (given the ego's acts, how can we ascertain that they are directed at objects?), and the realist version (given an object, what is that in which the object becomes its own image?).

3

A variant of the negation of the epistemological inquiry is the philosophy of Marx, extended at this point by various branches of twentieth-century Marxism, at the earliest moment probably by Stanisław Brzozowski. It demonstrates that man is unable to take on the position of a superhuman observer in relation to himself, that is, he cannot comprehend his own perception as a fragment of general evolution without falling into a vicious circle. Objects appear to man in the perspective of a practical endeavor as values, as objects for something. Consciousness is a self-knowing entity, while nature is the opposing member of a collective productive effort. Object and subject are known only as members of an opposition mutually relativized. There is no nonhistorical view of history; there is no truth which would be free from the conditions of its acquisition, which would not, in other words, be tied to the partial production by the species. Man cannot initiate cognition at a prehuman zero starting point; he is for himself the ultimate inevitable starting point.

Another version is contained in A. N. Whitehead's philosophy, which takes up the epistemological inquiry independently, without involving a historical perspective. In this version the images are in us, and we are in our own images. Experience is relativized in relation to the act of perception, that is, to the perceptual event which is a factor in every element or occurrence of experience. An event is thus partly described by a movement which grasps it perceptually. There is thus no distinction between "in the mind" and "outside the mind"; as in Avenarius's doctrine, there is no "interior." Cognition of nature is not an imagistic assimilation of ready-made material but a cognition "from within."

Merleau-Ponty's philosophy moves in a different direction, but it also questions the Cartesian-scholastic distinction, that is, it rejects the idea of objects puzzlingly entering into the field of subjectivity. The Cartesian *cogito* falsely divides consciousness into perception and the consciousness of perception, since this division is not contained in the act of perception. Perception is unconditionally primal: nothing precedes it. Hence questions regarding the genesis of perception cannot be put just like the question, whether perception reaches the world in itself, since the conception of such a world cannot be included in a sensible perceptual whole. In other words, man does not possess a ground outside himself on which he could both stand and know that he is standing there. He must start with himself; every other point of departure is the product of a derivative abstraction which cannot be made secure without returning to the human condition. Genetic questions relating to man falsely imply the possibility of a suprahuman observation point from which a relativized view of man is revealed. The relativization of man in scientific interpretations (his integration into a prehuman world in evolutionary theories, making perception dependent on the behavior of the organism in physiological investigations—that is, his reduction to nonhuman existence) is always derivative in relation to perception. Such reductions are inevitably imprisoned in humanity, and are therefore not valid if they pretend to have escaped that imprisonment. Those who undertake such reductions relativize humanity, thinking at the same time that they as humans have found a nonrelative point of view. In reality, since man cannot escape his humanity, he finds himself to be the only unconditioned reality. He knows that he is not an unconditioned reality; but he cannot articulate his own relativity without a vicious circle because perception is always primary, while within perception human existence and the world are given together in an unbreakable union. Consequently, we cannot explain the sense we give to objects and situations by referring to preconscious bodily needs, since we would then repeat the same invalid animalization of humanity. It is rather our needs that are the meaning which we give to our existence. Thus, Husserl's reduction plan, which would suspend existence in indecision, is false, as is the scientists' hidden belief that they can, free from human partiality, interpret that human partiality.

4

Merleau-Ponty's endeavor is perhaps the most radical attempt to remove the epistemological question. Avenarius's doctrine, which had a similar aim, gets entangled, when seen as a whole, in *petitio principii* characteristic of all biological relativists, as well as of pragmatists. For it assumes that the so-called cognitive acts may be understood fully as acts of restoring homeostasis to an organism which is constantly upset by stimuli from the environment. He interprets truth as a life-value, as a quality ascribed to experimental contents explicable in terms of preconditions under which the organism coexists with its environment—other qualities of experience (the aesthetic, for instance) being explicable in the same manner. On the other hand, in order to fix the position of cognitive activity and its situational definition, he refers to the established links between the behavior of the organism and the experience-contents, taking these connections as true in a popular rather than biologically determined sense of the word "true." The vicious circle of biological relativism has been revealed by Husserl in his *Logical Investigations,* and earlier still by Nietzsche; but the solution that Husserl proposed is illusory. He judged that we are able or will be able to reach a consciousness which would be a perfect transparency in relation to its contents and that we would be able to describe these contents free of habits fixed in common-sense thinking, even within the structures of the language we use; that, moreover, we shall one day be able to ask questions regarding the reality (that is, the genesis) of the objective field, on the assumption that the initial data contain no prejudices in this respect. Both these possibilities are however illusory. The first because the *eidos* of any given phenomenon would have to be grasped not only at a preverbal level, but also grasped in such a way that we would be convinced that our verbal and conceptual power had no influence on its formation. This supposition assumes the investigator returning to the *naiveté* of infancy, a return which is not only unbelievable but also impossible to assess even if it were performable. The second supposition sidesteps the issue. Initially, the transcendental reduction was only provisionally meant to suspend the question regarding the genesis or the source of reduced phenomena (the world in itself or the empirical ego), but in fact it made a retreat impossible, since there is no conceivable way which, from an analysis of neutralized contents, would have led back to their deneutralization. Whence come the data of consciousness it is impossible to deduce from their qualities, for we would previously need to know other similar genetic ties in order to be able to refer to their example and, by analogy, to infer, for instance, that contents are conditioned by the presence of objects or the presence of a psychological subject. In other words, the fundamental conditions for the appearance of data may be presupposed, but they cannot be established as a result of proof, if the proof starts with neutral data.

When existentialist philosophers—Heidegger, Sartre, and Merleau-Ponty—abandoned transcendental reduction in their reflections, this was the fruit of the understanding that reduction is irreversible and its temporariness illusory. The abandonment of reduction was meant to be the obverse of recognizing the intentionality of consciousness. The object given together with consciousness cancelled the Cartesian question. The perceived reality did not therefore return to a position of a preexisting field of assimilated externality; the external world could not be free of "situation"—it could not restore to consciousness the place of a thing coloured by the *species* of objects—it was part of the situation. At the same time, the union of the given and the intentional was irremovable.

5

The result of all these endeavors is a congruence of perspectives which emerge from such different philosophical traditions as phenomenology, existentialism, Marxism, and positivism. This congruity reveals itself at a crucial point: the validity of the epistemological inquiry. If it is a chimerical hope for man to shed his own skin; if the world is given only as a world endowed with meaning, and meaning is the outcome of man's practical project; if man is unable to understand himself by placing himself in a premeaningful, prehuman world (the history of the species, the unconscious body), because he cannot get to know the world without relating it to the human project—if therefore it is thus, the metaphysical inquiry and the epistemological inquiry are annulled at a stroke. Is this therefore the end of philosophy? The end of philosophy has already been proclaimed so often—either because it is impossible or because it is expendable or because it has fulfilled its task—that philosophers now prefer to leave such prophecies to cyberneticists; it is they who in our day have undertaken the task of announcing that the end of philosophy has arrived, and to this purpose they have marshaled arguments which this time are assuredly finally final.

Philosophers are inclined to think differently. They are also inclined to believe that the annulment of the epistemological and metaphysical inquiry cannot be performed once and for all, that the sense of these questions renews itself in successive historical situations, and hence the task of philosophy, even when negative and self-destructive, cannot stop.

They also think as follows. They think that even in circumstances where those who give up the hope that the world and human presence in it could be explained, where therefore every significance of the world is referred to the human project, the task of philosophy is to articulate these meanings to the best of its ability, although it does not undertake to provide them with metaphysical significance.

And they think yet more. They think that the incomprehensibility of the world and the absence of a potency which would actualize itself in human history and make it meaningful with reference to the prehistorical background reveal themselves within the restriction imposed by experience. In other words, experience (that is, perception, both of whose elements are invariably given together) does not offer philosophical reflection any transcendental hopes. But philosophy must be conscious of those sources from which human history unremittingly draws the strength to renew those hopes; it must therefore know the historical reasons which bring back to life metaphysical beliefs, even though it is unable, within its own rigors, to opt for these reasons. When we step outside the rigors of philosophy, we move into faith; but philosophy, as thinking about culture, has been charged with the task of investigating the meaning of every faith. Within the rigors of its boundaries, philosophy is unable to accept faith, but it cannot exclude the possibility that faith inescapably contributes to the flowering of culture. Within their own profession, philosophers can only interpret faith, referring its meaning to nontranscendable *humanitas*. And although philosophers do not differ from other people, and have not been deprived of that aspect of human existence which intentionally refers to mythical realities, nevertheless they will not turn it into a reason for thought, and its presence cannot serve them as justifying a philosophical move beyond *humanitas*. Thus, philosophers may awaken sensitivities to the meaning of acts which go beyond philosophy and scientific thought, even though it is not possible to justify such sensitivities as values other than by turning them into relative, historical, and genetic human values. Philosophers are tools with which culture defines itself in its rights to move beyond philosophy, although philosophers do not grant such rights other than by relativizing them in relation to culture.

These are the three possible applications of philosophy in conditions under which philosophy has condemned its own instruments which once, as it thought, allowed it to move beyond the horizon of perception.

6

If, then, philosophical critique cancels the traditional inquiry regarding the presence of things beyond perception, as a question incapable of an answer, or even incapable of a proper formulation, it cannot nevertheless remove the need which animates that inquiry. There is a need to have at one's disposal a conceptual tool referring to existence in a nonconditioned sense (that is, of existence which cannot be reduced to the belonging to a set) and every satisfaction of that need is a mythopoeic task. Any philosophy which does not wish to take account of the results of the critique applied to the epistemological question takes on a mythopoeic task.

And it appears that our culture cannot truly do without mythological solutions of the epistemological question. The observation that a solipsistic position is an option which is logically permissible but culturally barren is undoubtedly true. But a barren option for common sense and scientific reason is also the point of view which relies on the rigor of experience, and on that account rejects all answers to the question which assumes a distinction between consciousness and objects, a consciousness which precedes the perceptual situation. In other words, this distinction, although inadmissible within the rigor of experience, cannot be removed from common-sense and scientific reason. It is necessary, because without its aid I am unable to understand myself situationally, that is, to understand myself as placed among objects which are totally different from me; I cannot therefore name myself as different from the world—that is, I cannot give an account of the irresistible sense of self-identification. This sense may be confusing to the inconceivable observational position, which arises above the horizon of perception, but it cannot be removed. Thus, both the justification of my own identity and the justification of the human community, by referring it to the common environment of objects, requires the mythical option which is contained in accepting the category of existence in a nonconditional sense, that is, contained in posing and answering the epistemological question. I must understand myself as an element of an already given situation, I must therefore believe that I can understand the presence of the world as precisely an existent. The category of existence in the nonconditioned sense cannot, of course, be the work of a successive abstractions, as was imagined by empiricists confident in the natural validity of the Aristotelian hierarchy or predicates; for it is clear that stages of abstraction are stages in the scope of sets, but in no way do we reach a position where the act of existence reveals itself. At this point Gilson's critique is undoubtedly correct; what is incorrect is his speculation that philosophy is capable of manipulating the category of the act of existence without drawing upon mythological resources. Philosophical abandonment of classical epistemology is an abandonment in favor of myth whose absence in our culture it is impossible to imagine.

3

MYTH IN THE REALM OF VALUES

1

Undoubtedly the needs which turn people towards self-relativization in myth are to a certain extent inimical to freedom. That is because the yearning to be rooted in a world organized by myth aims at defining oneself in a given and experienced order of values; it is a desire to step outside oneself into an order in which one treats oneself as an object with a designated sphere of possibilities, as a thing, as filling in a space in a structure which—virtually, at least—is already complete. As a participant in myth, I am unable to treat the succeeding moments of my own existence as an absolute beginning, and I therefore concur at reducing my own freedom and try to take up a point of view from which I am wholly visible. This point of view is not only suprapersonal—that is, not only one which destroys me in my origins—but also suprahuman; for it is not only I who surrender to the objectifying gaze in which I identify with that transcending movement—I surrender the whole humanity to that gaze. For it is clear that independently of possible personal particularizations to which myth is subject at each absorption by an individual, it can be absorbed by that individual only when he gives it a universally valid, generally binding, and universally human meaning. A myth can be accepted only to the extent that, with regard to a particular point of view, it becomes a kind of constraint, binding equally the whole group, be it humanity at large or a tribe, in which the individual participates. Thus, a value-creating myth implies a surrender of freedom, since it imposes a ready-made model and a surrender of the absolute primacy of one's humanity, since it attempts to set humanity, and therefore the historical community, in an unconditionally primary dimension and to refer it to a nontemporal order.

Thus, myth cannot be justified within the boundaries of a consciousness which decides to reject the prehuman horizon of perception as illusory, and which does not believe in an escape from history. Nor can it be justified within a consciousness which establishes its own freedom as unlimited with reference to every momentary segment of its own existence, that is, a consciousness which doggedly attempts to disown a reified status.

2

But the struggle toward a perfect salvation from "reification" appears futile, as is the pursuit of the ideal of a total self-constitution. Philosophers such as Stirner and Nietzsche, who had attempted to sketch out such an ideal, were able to do so by leaving things unsaid. For this ideal depends on conceiving a situation of life's constant discontinuity, which originates at birth and at each segment of one's own time and at each point starts from a zero position. My acts of bestowing meanings on things and events, acts of the so-called establishment of values, would arise from each successive unconditioned spontaneity and would on each occasion raise me to the position of Creator who calls his universe to renewed life from nothingness, as in the theology of the Mutakallimun, which seemingly at each moment compels God to banish the cosmos into nothingness and to raise it up from nothingness, since the world's time is discontinuous and atomistically structured. The unconditioned beginning which I ascribe to myself in this fantasy makes it impossible to ask, "Why should I ascribe this particular meaning to things?" or "Why should I establish these particular values?" This is because a creation out of nothing cannot allow the questioning of its reasons. But let us assume that I do not wish to stop at the vague phraseology of "creating values," and am considering what practical consequences should flow from my belief in the possibility of my own perfect self-constitution. Were my behavior reducible to systematic violations of generally accepted values, it would be missing its target, since it would not be a spontaneity but a voluntary acquiescence at a complete negative dependence on this general currency. Nor can I by definition refer to it positively: I am forbidden to refer even to my own identity, since I cannot accept that that which I was a moment previously should bind me in any way at this moment. My own continuity, experienced as such, is for me neither value-creating nor meaning-designating: it creates neither obligations nor understanding. So what does creation, relieved of reasons, amount to? If it is not connected with the order of obligations, and if the sense of obligation does not bind it either, it is not creation, but a causal dependence on the order of my body and my empirical ego. It is therefore an apparent spontaneity, which depends solely on removing the barrier established earlier by internalized culture, that is, by the totality of impulses of preconscious existence between my empirical existence and my behavior. The zero freedom of my being in the world of values, springing from the assumed discontinuity, is an unfreedom in relation to the causal determinants of my body. The perfection of my humanity turns by force of a dialectical trap into a prehuman perfection, a return to animality—not a dialectical return, but a second fall into a precultural nature, a fall which anyway is unperformable in practice except in the euphoric fantasies of "lofty barbarians." This is not the intention of those who were proclaiming the creation of values as an ideal aimed at every single individual, but a consequence of their call having been unknowingly suppressed.

3

It is thus apparent that the absolute salvation from the "reified" form of existence, were it possible in practice, would still all anxieties stirred by the situation of responsibility, since such a situation is annulled by the general decree which wipes out existing values at a stroke. Whoever believes that he has issued this decree does not create good and evil, but rather refuses to admit the difference between good and evil. He who confines himself to choosing among existing values succumbs to the restrictions of reified existence.

4

There is, however, an essential reason contained in calls which demand that I should distinguish myself as an object among objects, from myself as a self-related reality; which therefore demand that I distinguish my de facto dependence on the atmosphere of values which I breathe in and which I find within myself, from the potentialities of my self-constituting struggles with the imposing presence of the existing order. There is, in other words, essential reason in the attempts to grant the fact of creativity such a meaning as would reveal the discontinuity contained in it—its quality of indeterminacy. The need to have a sense of discontinuity, together with the awareness that a complete discontinuity is a mirage or a demotion, gives rise to a questioning situation which needs to be overcome.

If creation, therefore, unbound in the illusion of the creator by any imperative of an existing order of values, can only be either a hallucinatory vibration of a vacuum or an agreement to reenter the imprisonment of a causal dependence upon prehuman impulses; if it cannot leave behind any trace which would be a true value (since that trace would have negated the creator's intention, would have been a fixed sediment binding upon further creativity, and would therefore be that creation's prison); if creation from zero therefore has to perish at the moment of its birth for fear of negating its own creative nature; if all this is so, is the alternative to this solipsistic illusion the abandonment of the idea of creation—a willing assent to our submissiveness vis àvis the just given order of values? Is there a dilemma and is it inevitable: do I either identify in imagination with my own complete spontaneity, resigned to the continuing perishing of my own creation; or do I accept the situation of a thing, aware that being rooted in the world means an identification with its order? But if the dilemma is not inevitable, is there a third alternative capable of overcoming it?

The awakening of reflection which situates me in the world of meanings and which stimulates the demand that each meaning given to events should be *mine* (that is, a meaning decreed by me) appears only when I am able to understand the signs of my culture, when, as it were, I become a domesticated animal, absorbing the values of this culture as my own attributes. It is thus impossible that my revolt against culture should ever become total, since it would demand such a disruption of continuity that I would have removed the totality of its meanings from the level of internalization. I would, in other words, have ceased to understand them, not just ceased to value them, because I cease to understand a value if I cannot, to whatever degree, accept it as my own, a situation quite different from understanding propositions which I can simultaneously comprehend and totally reject. At the root of every revolt, therefore, is an element of that same culture which I am rejecting; only in the name of something which I have not created do I usurp the desire to create.

But the values of my culture cannot be jointly implemented and kept intact. An overwhelming proportion of my acts consists of compromises in which a partial or fragmentary saving of a value occurs at the expense of saving it as a whole, and this loss is incurred in order partially to save another value. Daily life consists of such accommodations. The degree of acceptable compromise—the extent of possible abandonment of a partial actualization of a value for the sake of another value—is not clearly defined by the norms of my culture. And this indeterminacy is the greater, the greater is the potential of my culture's flowering. Although the material is fixed, the successive delineation of these boundaries contains infinite possibilities of variation. We call these variations "creation" when the fixed boundaries of complementary regressions cannot be derived from that tradition. Creation thus means the introduction of novelty, though it is not possible as a step beyond the values of my culture, but only as a change in the methods of their complementary accommodations. The most extreme nihilist may attempt to escape from the forms of inherited values, but such an escape cannot succeed. At the heart of the explosion, which seems to blow the inheritance apart, the explosive material always contains a portion of the inherited reserves.

5

But an objection arises: this situation does not provide any reason for justifying myth, since if I cannot succeed even at the extremity of my revolt in escaping the inheritance of values, it surely does not follow that I must treat these values as the nonhistoric data of human existence. I can tell myself: a complete escape is impossible, since the values I was brought up on limit all choices; nevertheless I am free to adhere to the following two convictions: "This is good" and "I believe that this is good, because this is the way I was brought up, and whatever I may do, I shall do constrained by the circumstances of the influence which life has exerted upon me."

But can I retain two convictions together? Can I maintain a belief in something being good or evil, while treating that belief exclusively as a factual circumstance to be explained causally? It seems that when I believe in something, aware that my belief is based on the ready-made historical legacy, there is a crucial difference between my belief whose content is a certain event (I believe for instance that I was born on a certain day at a certain time) and when it is an affirmation of value. In the first instance I do not feel the burden of any incoherence which encumbers the second. For when I try to turn myself completely into an object of my own perception (an explicable thing), and when in the same perception I refer my own awareness of values to my own biography for explanation, the meaning of the words in which I express this awareness immediately changes. Claiming that something is a value, and being at the same time mindful of the reasons explaining my affirmation, I immediately cease to claim that something is a value, because my claim acquires a single meaning incapable of expansion: "I experience this being as a value." In other words, I am describing my own awareness without finding a bridge which would lead me beyond the psychological object, with which I identify myself, towards the value which I am claiming. The causal explanation of the experience of value forbids my expression of this experience as a conviction regarding values, that is, it cancels the content of the experience, leaving just the psychological fact. Otherwise my explanation would have had to be: "This is not a value but I believe it to be a value." Since, however, the judgment "This is not a value," affirmed with conviction, is equivalent to the judgment "I am convinced that it is not a value," my readiness for self-explanatory interpretation compels me to accept the following judgment: "I am convinced that this is not a value, but I am convinced that it is a value."

This conclusion is not immediately apparent, hence it is possible to hide the contradiction and to attempt to uphold jointly the convictions which imply it. But such attempts are always based on bad faith, which can be seen in those who try to save the scientistic standpoint and to deprive their own experience of values of all content, save that possessed by psychological facts.

It is of course possible to move further towards self-objectivization without contradiction. It is possible to declare: "Nothing is a value, but schooling has produced in me approving and disapproving forms of reaction to specific situations." Should I really succeed in applying this interpretation, I would be seeing my own valuing reactions as conditioned responses, regarding whose propriety or impropriety it is impossible to inquire.

I am not aware that anyone has ever managed to transform his own consciousness in this spirit, that is, to objectify completely his own moral self-knowledge and to reduce it to a causally explicable fact. What is certain, however, is that a society is inconceivable in which the transmission of values would follow this principle, that is, a society aiming at producing a universalized scientistic attitude among its members. Education in such a society would need to adopt the following pattern: "You must know that nothing is either good or evil, but I am teaching you that some things are good and some are evil, in order to induce in you conditioned reflexes which are useful for the maintenance of solidarity in communal life which is neither good nor evil but must be seen as good."

The natural social self-defense against education so conceived (that is, an education which gives up authority or employs authority, while at the same time proclaiming its fictitiousness) is understandable. Since an effective inheritance of values is always the work of authority, and every act of emancipation from authority may arise only in the name of values absorbed thanks to authority, a scientistic upbringing is therefore an absurd utopia. Those who claim freedom from authority speak in bad faith. Whoever claims to be able to survive a conviction about the conditioned-reflex nature of all values speaks in bad faith.

But values inherited under a binding functioning of authority are being inherited in their mythical form; they are not being inherited as information about social or psychological facts (that this or that happens to be thought valuable) but precisely as information regarding what is or is not a value. The idols of the tribe govern in an inescapable manner: a complete emancipation from them springs from a tyranny of another illusion. Universal godlessness is a utopia. Myths that teach us that something simply is good or evil cannot be avoided if humanity is to survive.

6

But isn't the word "myth" being used improperly here? Since the question concerns the usage of the word, it can be decided by stipulation, so long as we are able to give the word a clear content. I call "mythical" every conviction which not only transcends finite experience in the sense that it does not describe it (since every hypothesis in this sense steps beyond experience) but also in the sense that it relativizes every possible experience, referring it to realities whose verbal description cannot in principle be tied logically with verbal descriptions of experience. In other words, the realities of the mythical order can explain nothing about the realities of experience, nor, even less, be derivable from them. They are also nonoperative: they do not enable us to predict or explain anything.

The universe of values is a mythical reality. To the extent that we endow with values the elements of experience, situations, and things, we perceive them as participating in that reality which unconditionally transcends the totality of possible experience. We know what reality is by referring finite experiences to it, with the awareness that no finite experience reaches it. We therefore know it as the precondition of all experience, of all history, of all humanity, all individual life, all human social coexistence. If we consider that we know that reality as part of history, as a quality of humanity, and as a quality of culture—what we actually do know is not it, but the *facts* of valuation. All experiencing reveals to us values as cultural facts, capable of classification and explanation, suitable for arrangement into so-called functional laws. Within experience, value imprisoned in its relativity is a cultural fact. Despite Husserl's hopes, there is no eidetic experience of values which would turn our valuations into *knowledge*. Value is a myth; it is *transcendens*.

7

Similarly, in our *understanding of law* as an obligation applying to all equally, there is hidden an appeal to a mythical foundation. As regards its particular form, law can of course be explained in terms of historical conditions; in fact, among civilizing institutions none can be explained so convincingly in historical terms. It can also be *justified* by a theory of social contract: as an external pressure which individuals encounter whose rationale is the guarantee of mutual security of all by the limitation of each. All justifications of law tacitly refer to Hobbesian assumptions regarding the organic conflict of interests. When Kant declares that the law would perform its function equally well in a society of Satans, he is assuming its purely repressive value, and when he says additionally that the law is necessary for the regulation of human relationships, he assumes that the threat of repression is the condition of human cooperation and solidarity. He therefore assumes the notion of human nature as evil, necessarily condemned to abide in the shadow of force. If, however, one were to accept these assumptions as a factual description, and if one were even to go further and follow Sartre in declaring that all human bonds are constituted in rivalry and conflict, that therefore an existential communication is in principle impossible, the presence of myth in law, even when conceived as naked repression, cannot be eliminated. For, from the principle which explains the necessity of the law, no rule defining its content follows; not even that most general one, according to which legal commands apply equally to all participants in the legal community: neither the principle of *nullum crimen sine lege,* nor *lex retro non agit,* and so on. The reason for any materially designated legal rule must be different from the reason for the presence of law as such. The last of the rules mentioned above is compatible with a law which establishes an irrational privilege, as well as with a law which accepts the principle of equality; and also with a law whose source is the whim of a petty tyrant, as well as with law derived from freely expressed will by representatives of the whole community.

It is of course easy to say that there is no legal rule which is binding in all known cultures (with the exception, perhaps, of incest, which in any event is variously defined). From this observation the inevitability of our acceptance of the legally equivalent relativity of all judicial systems does not inevitably follow; also, were it the case that a collection of legal rules were present in all cultures (there is such a universal presence of logical rules) one could not from this purely factual universality conclude that certain legal principles bind unconditionally and belong to the essence of legal ties. In a word, from the observation of cultural and historical similarity or dissimilarity of legal rules, no conclusion follows which is essential to the question: Is a distinction between "bad" and "good" law possible? Or: Are all laws the expression of a random distribution of forces in a community? Or: Are perhaps certain legal systems better than others as embodiments of the real obligation (which precedes history) which weighs on the coexistence of people in large groups?

Nor, as phenomenologists would wish, is this question answerable through eidetic reflection, which would reveal the self-standing nature of the legal bond, so as to derive from it fundamental rules which are truly valid, which determine the framework of all concrete legislation, or which make it possible to find a court of appeal for every legislation so as to judge it as good or evil. Our ancestor the troglodyte did not discover on the walls of his cave the Rights of Man written up by God; but neither did he write them as a consequence of generalizing his experiences; the bill was simply decreed by his descendants; and should their descendants in turn wish to annul it and replace it with a declaration of general lawlessness, no one would be able to blame them for being at fault in the cognitive sense of the word. A question regarding unconditioned obligation is not answerable as part of knowledge. Nevertheless, it is needed. We wish to know whether the Roman legal order, whose general principles continue to define the European juridical culture, is an accidental result, or the initial historical revelation of that which, in the legal bond as such, *ought* to be present. We wish it not only in order to find assurance for our own opinions about law, not only in order to rid ourselves of the sense of being absolute legislators in matters concerning the basic norms of legal order, and not only so that a certain institution, which humanity found ready-made, should lead us beyond ourselves and enable us to escape responsibility for the laws which we create. This is because total responsibility, that is, one which does not regard any value as a nonarbitrary reality, is a responsibility for nothing at all, is therefore an imaginary responsibility. A foundation of law which antedates legislation and inscribes each item of legislation into restrictions is also a collection of values; it might be the value of equality or the value of privilege, the value of reciprocity in external obligations, the value of life in a social order from which it is clear what to expect, and so on. If every value is a free decision without antecedent orienteering points, responsibility for each and every decision is a baseless fantasy, since every decision appears equally good. This is the situation in Sartre's philosophy in which "responsibility for the whole world" means the annulment of all responsibility, while the anxiety regarding one's own decision is speculative fiction which no one who was taking seriously the assumptions of this doctrine could have entertained. In a word, the validity of a legal order shares in the weakness of every collection of values to which a purely factual, cultural, historical, or psychological mode of existence is ascribed. We are not justified in holding on to any legal order by claiming that it embodies real values of coexistence, if we are not able to refer it to a mythological realm of valuations. (In saying all this we are probably simply reiterating the ideas set out in Book 4 of Plato's *Laws*.) But if we persist in our obstinacy and insist on defending the purely factual status of legislation, we sink into the same antinomy that we have already noted—that antinomy born of affirming values which simultaneously are considered accidental.)

8

The mythical consciousness is ubiquitous, although normally poorly revealed. If it is present in every understanding of the world as endowed with values, it is also present in every understanding of history as meaningful.

Understanding history as meaningful or understanding it *tout court,* is the same as being able to refer events to that which is either a teleologically bounded order, or to that which, even if it is not his goal, is nevertheless man's destiny in history. For an event in history is not intelligible because the motives of its participants are comprehensible; this intelligibility is neither a necessary nor a sufficient condition of understanding the event as a fragment of history. For an event to be intelligible—that is, meaningful—it is not sufficient (nor is it necessary) for it to be interpretable with reference to some empirically discoverable regularities in the historical process, assuming that such regularities are ever capable of being reliably discovered. For in such a case, it would simply be explicable analogously to natural events. Then also natural events (for instance, natural disasters, climatic changes, plagues, births, and deaths), which are significant in the course of historical events, would themselves have had to be meaningful as historical events, such meaningfulness, of course, not being enhanced by their explicability in the order of nature. Analogously, the knowledge of the psychological conditions of its occurrence does not contribute to the meaningfulness of a historical event. From the point of view of historical understanding, an event which is an outcome of a free decision does not differ from an avalanche.

Thus, the meaning of an event is not revealed through its conditions (be they motivational or nonhuman), but because the event may be referred either to the goal at which the historical course aims (namely, as a factor in approaching that goal or in moving away from it) or to our human destiny which is either being actualized in history or demands such actualizations. "Goal," in the precise sense of the word, requires an intention, that is, a self-knowing project of prehistoric providence. The presence of destiny or potentiality, which either claims its rights or sets empirical existence in motion aimed at the congruence of existence with essence, is not in need of a providential project. Nevertheless, it requires a mythical court of appeal which antedates all historicity, making it relative, and therefore demands that every event should be understood as in accord or not in accord with our human destiny.

However, our human destiny is neither a reality included in historical material nor a hypothesis which could have emerged from the gathering of the material. It is a rule for the understanding of events, and such a rule is valid to the extent that the nontemporal set of demands which codefine humanity precedes all human historical existence.

But only under this condition are we allowed meaningfully to say: these situations are inhuman and demand to be annulled; these conditions are hostile to humanity and must be wiped out from our world. Only under this condition are we allowed to assert that we know the meaning of the words "liberation of man," "damnation of man," and "alienation of man." Only under this condition have we the right to demand that man should find himself, or demand for him freedom, contentment, and self-realization.

And yet, all of Marx's thought is an unceasing demand for the restoration to man of his humanity. He demands the universal emancipation of humanity, going beyond political emancipation; he demands the elimination of inhuman conditions, and the humanization of things; he demands that historical reality should coalesce with human dignity.

And yet Husserl detects in the stages of the development of the human mind a gradual rising towards culture which will bring about—perhaps in infinity—the identity of historical culture with culture par excellence, that is, will fulfill our human destiny by introducing the imperative *eidos* of humanity into factual existence.

And yet Hegel knows the manner in which, in the agony of real history, the spirit seeking embodiment acquires a voice.

Meanwhile Freud says that there is no law on the strength of which man is destined to happiness.

Meanwhile Sartre declares that there are no inhuman situations.

In fact, if man is what he is in the repeated agony of empirical duration, in his zoological determinations, and nothing above that—there is no law which destines him to happiness. In fact, if the *eidos* of humanity which precedes factual existence is not present, there are no inhuman situations, that is, those that contradict the idea of man.

But each time I raise my voice against the conditions which insult human dignity; each time, even unknowingly, I project my own voice towards reasons which are rooted in knowledge of what human dignity *truly* is, then each time I demonstrate that I know what a realized man would be, or what the demand to be human is.

But each time I demand freedom, I reveal the secret of humanity, since I reveal that man *ought* to have freedom.

Whereas in terms of history enclosed within the boundaries of events, be they frozen into laws, be they explained causally, man is not owed anything, man is not called to anything, humanity does not demand anything, man is neither a true, less true, or an untrue human being. He is what he happens to be.

And from an empirical point of view, history is bounded in just this manner. It therefore contains no reasons on the strength of which I could claim anything for humanity or in its name. Therefore each call I make, each demand upon history, each valuation of an event, either has no reason or has reasons within myth, that is, within humanity antedating history.

It is therefore also through myth present in us that what

happens, happens; that is why at every moment our practical dwelling in history renews its energy from the root of myth. Thanks to it we gain the right to impose a meaning upon events and a right to a voice for or against whatever happens to be the case.

And if myth is a secondary projection of our practical intention, whose role is to secure and justify that intention, then, nevertheless, were we to be certain that it is such a projection, we would be unable to accept it. The moment we know it, or think that we know it, our right to have a voice and our right to impose meaning upon events are taken away from us. That is why factual history requires myth, and hence we have no right to regard ourselves as fully the creators of myth, but rather as its discoverers.

9

The presence of myth in art is more difficult to grasp, but it is no less real than in the areas just touched upon. A work of art can of course be an intended projection of a myth which is already present in the collective imagination. But that is not what I have in mind. Rather, I want to point out that that which is common to the creation of art and its perception is rooted differently in the mythical layers of our coexistence: art is a way of forgiving the world for its evil and chaos. Forgiveness does not in any way mean an accord with evil or a decision not to stand up to it. Neither does it signify a justification of evil, nor does it have to motivate a theodicy. It is not a debilitating affect aimed at possible and future evil. Art may also forgive the world its evil when it tightens its grip on a stone and lifts it. Forgiveness has another meaning. Art organizes the perception of evil and chaos and absorbs them into an understanding of life in such a way that the presence of evil and chaos becomes the possibility of my initiative towards the world which carries its own good and evil. For this to come about, art has to reveal in the world what is not directly perceptible in it, namely, the hidden charm of its ugliness, the veiled humpiness of its beauty, the ridiculousness of its sublimity, the misery of its opulence, and the preciousness of its wretchedness—in other words, to unravel all the secret strands round which the empirical qualities grow and which turn these qualities into elements of our fall or our pride. The crystallization of the world in art is always unjust, because infinitely biased, since it constrains me to acknowledge that the whole world is either anger or frustrated desire, or is wholly peace, or wholly awaiting an explosion. There is no quality, however fleeting, of my experiencing the world, which could not be petrified in art as a challenging—since fixed—naming of Being. A work of art, just because it endures, is boundlessly partial, therefore intolerant, since on every occasion it excludes all other possibilities of naming Being. But this intolerance always contains the hope that my partial experience will be capable of turning into a value which in the movement of my initiative I shall be able to place in opposition to the world as given. For this hope to arise truly, my understanding of art—and therefore also its creation—must refer to the mythopoeic power which I carry, since only thanks to that power do I dare express my own organization of the world as a world made up of noncongruent and mutually conflicting value-qualities.

4

MYTH IN LOGIC

1

The assumption that we perhaps find most offensive is that mythical intuitions are present and irremovable in our understanding of the rules of logic in which the paramountcy of reason is experienced most forcefully. But it is precisely the sense of this sovereignty which, when inspected more closely, reveals the radiation of the mythical consciousness upon the imperatives of our mental labors. And this is how it comes about.

Taking the matter schematically, we can record four principal recommendations as to the meaning which is to be assigned to the assertions of logic.

Nineteenth-century psychologism, criticized by Husserl (and in part already by Frege and Bolzano) recommended that these assertions be treated as empirical regularities discoverable in human mental behaviour. In the extreme version, the compulsion that we experience in the face of the rules of proceeding from proposition to proposition would simply be the result of a hypothetical causal nexus, on the strength of which a factually accepted judgment of a given form creates a factual impossibility of rejecting some other judgment of a given form—that very judgment which on the basis of whatever logical norms is derivable from the first. The laws of reason are then descriptions of certain recurring connections between facts arising in man's psychic or nervous system.

2

Husserl criticizes this doctrine as spelling the ruin of all assumptions upon which European spiritual culture is based, and as a complete distortion of the meaning which we truly assign to our logic. In fact, psychologism forces us to the following unappetizing conclusion: the whole of our knowledge is ruled by principles which have no attribute of the norms binding all thought, thinking as such, nor do they guarantee that one has to think in just this manner; they simply describe how our brain functions in a particular area of its activity. They therefore allow the suggestion that a differently constructed brain thinks according to a different logic, while ours is in this sense contingent, that is, is relative to the genetic qualities of our bodily constitution. According to this assumption our whole world-picture, built on centuries of scientific endeavors, and supported invariably upon the constraints of one and the same mental discipline, is a collection of instruments assimilated by the species for an effective manipulation of things, and we would be inquiring about its "truth" or cognitive justification with as much right as we would regarding the "truth" of a hammer or a spring. Psychological relativism is unable to accommodate the assumption that scientific thought is something other than a physiological reaction, that it not only equips us better to control the world, but also reveals to us the world in truth. It cannot therefore allow a discontinuity between the animal watchfulness of our bodies and the passion of our intellectual explorations. This relativism conceals the classical error of *hysteron proteron* of all skeptics who try to use the instruments of proof to demonstrate the vacuity of all proof; psychologists describe logic as a "life" mechanism, and in so doing they employ the rules of logic which they regard as an organ of valid argument; in order to deny it rational justification in principle, they rely on it as rationally justified. They are therefore entangled in a vicious and baseless circle. Of course, there is an escape, but it requires a departure from the ruts of empirical habit. The propositions of logic are not about how our brain works in practice; nor do they imply any real experiences, or any psychological facts. They are norms that constrain unconditionally and precede all factual thought; they are not about *how we think,* but about *how we ought to think,* in order to think properly. They contain no reference to time and remain valid irrespective of whether we exist, whether anybody thinks, or whether the world exists. They belong to a world of ideal bonds, a world which reveals its necessity to the radical perception of a thinker freed from the prejudices of biological empiricism. This world contains neotic conditions a priori of all concrete thought, and these conditions are recognizable immediately as inescapable, once we come to understand them.

3

There are other possible nonpsychological ways of understanding logic besides the one outlined by Husserl. We may, for example, in accordance with the doctrine of logical empiricism, accept the constraints of logical rules as the outcome of meaning which language itself imposes upon words. For instance, employing the mode of speech introduced by Ajdukiewicz, we say that the meaning of a rule given by *modus ponens* is reducible to the following: Whoever accepts the proposition in the form "If p then q," and also asserts the proposition "p," and would at the same time deny the proposition "q," would thereby demonstrate that he does not understand the expression "If . . . then" in the sense ascribed to it by the English language. In other words, the validity of a particular rule of deduction—for example, the one expressed in *modus ponens,* coupled with a sense of constraint experienced when it is understood—derives from linguistic circumstances, namely, the meaning of logical constants fixed in a given natural language or in the conventions of the artificial languages of deductive systems. Every logical structure is here derivative in relation to the conventions of the language in which it is being expressed. The genesis of meanings fixed in just such a manner is a question of fact, which does not belong to epistemological investigation but rather to the history or psychology of language. The tacit assumption in this explanation is that the origin of linguistic conventions is not relevant to the epistemological valuation of judgments and rules recognized on the basis of these conventions.

4

Piaget's doctrine of genetic epistemology is a partial return to the psychological interpretation. In reality, this is not epistemology, but a developmental psychology of intelligence, which within the framework of its experimental constraints cannot allow any epistemological inquiry, but transforms them all *a limine* into

psychological questions. From the point of view of this doctrine there are behavioral equivalents of logical operations, preceding their general linguistic articulation in a person's development, but essential for such an articulation to occur at a later stage. Unlike earlier psychologistic theorists, Piaget posits no innate logical constructs. Nor does he posit transcendental norms of thinking. The very need for proof, for justifying one's own position, springs from a need to persuade, and therefore from social contacts at the level of discourse. The gradual formation of thought-norms is the outcome of the combined influence of social conditions, practical operations on the objects in early childhood, and of speech which, while admittedly it does not impose logical schemas as a sufficient condition, does nevertheless enable such schemas to pass into a sphere of wholly conscious applicability. In the course of a mutual adaptation between ready-made cognitive schemas (there always are some that we encounter when we conduct our investigations) which attempt to assimilate new perceptions and those very perceptions (which do change the schemas gradually and themselves succumb to their pressure) the mind progresses towards equilibrium, whose abstract expression establishes itself among others as socially accepted laws of logic. The principle of contradiction, if it is to become a law of thought, requires interpersonal communication in which it becomes a condition of solidarity. (This looks like a repetition of the old idea of Łukasiewicz that the principle of contradiction should be treated as a moral norm.) In the early phases of its development a child is incapable of understanding a transitive relation, that is, when it knows that $A > B$ and $B > C$, it is unable on this basis to reach the conclusion $A > C$. Nevertheless, in its practical behavior, it is capable of discovering asymmetrical relationships and consequently will in time mentally grasp the general principle which simultaneously both describes and regulates it. In sum, despite certain ambiguities, arising undoubtedly from ignoring Kant's and Husserl's warning that epistemological inquiries must be distinguished from all experimentally decidable genetic inquiries, Piaget's thought clearly focuses on genetic relativism: the rules of logic do not possess the validity which precedes their effective constitution in thought. Similarly, as regards arithmetical and geometrical propositions: it is not the case, to put it crudely, that "in his very nature" man

has two eyes, a truth which he discovers when he acquires the ability to employ the concept "two"; duality as a property present in the world is born together with the presence of "two" in man's thought, behavior, and speech. (A baby undoubtedly has two eyes before it knows the fact, but it has them *because* of the culture of the adults, not by reference to a system of natural numbers subsisting in a prehuman world.) Neither logic nor arithmetic demand experience as a court of appeal in order to be justified. But their link with experience does not depend solely on occasional causality. Experience brings forth the conceptual tools thanks to which the rules of logic *become* truth, that is, become *tout court*.

5

When we confront these four interpretations, we notice at once that the first and the fourth do not answer the epistemological question but simply invalidate it, while the third invalidates the genetic question. In both its variants psychologism obliges us to abandon any supposition that there are any norms preceding the factual workings of our mind which constrain those workings; there is no a priori ethic of thought. Within the bounds of experience, regarding whose ultimate validity it is impossible to inquire, the subject and object, factual thought and its normative regulation, are graspable only in a mutual coupling, and neither is absolutely primary in relation to the other. The experience is autarkic and cannot have a ground. The sense of logical rules is such that they either describe factual regularities of our mental labors (for instance, "It is impossible to utter simultaneously with conviction two directly contradictory propositions") or, if they relate to propositions as such rather than to our thoughts, they owe their validity to the practical need of interpersonal communication and technological effectiveness. As to why technological effectiveness demands a certain determined and not an arbitrary logic—that is a question which springs from metaphysical habits and is bereft of empirical sense. Consequently, we have no right to believe that logic weighs as an *obligation* upon our thought. And scientific replication of the world is a link in a chain of the collective labors of generations desiring to accommodate themselves in this world. Cognitive valuation has no other horizon of

legitimate interest apart from this one, designated by our need to communicate in a collective adaptation of ourselves to things and of things to us.

Canceling in turn, in the spirit of logic empiricism, the value of the genetic inquiry (as a question of fact) in the interpretation of logic, and confining ourselves to its maximally precise description as a collection of tautologies designated by the meanings of logical constants embedded in natural languages, we convert logical rules into norms devoid of reasons outside contingent linguistic usage: "Use the negation sign in such a manner that its use excludes the possibility of a simultaneous acceptance of propositions p and not $=p$." Such would be the sense ascribed to the principle of contradiction. To the question, why?, we can only reply that this is the sense that natural languages attach to the negation sign. There is no further explanation beyond this factual information. Is there in the nature of thinking a property which constrains all natural languages to constructs from which precisely this and always the same logic must arise? This question transcends the bounds of possible experience.

But an answer to this question finally settles the meaning which every logical rule possesses. By invalidating it, we turn logic into a linguistic fact—such is language. That is why the positivistic explanation which abandons the genetic question endows the forms of thought with the same factual status as a psychological explanation which is confined to the genetic question. (It may even be that logic in this formulation is even more suspect of contingency, since for its validation it is forced to refer not to man's genetic properties but to natural languages which in every single case may validate the norms of thought; the congruence of these assertions in various languages is also contingent, and in any event must appear surprising.)

That is why among the four accounts I have described, only Husserl's attempts to save logic as a real obligation which the mind *discovers* and which it is *obliged* to obey. However, this ability to save it depends on myth whose mythic character he refuses to accept; the myth of transcendental consciousness which, liberated from all factual prejudices, is able to take control of the eidetic necessities of Being, and is therefore also able to uncover the *eidos* of thinking in its irresistible law-making which precedes all factual thought.

Husserl's myth, constructed like a fortress against the destructive skepticism of psychologists and psychologizing epistemologists, historians, and historicists, is a repetition of the myth which Plato had built against the Sophists, perhaps with greater degree of self-knowledge regarding its mythic status. The realm of ideas was seen as a discovery of a universe which makes possible the revelation of a nonfactual necessity contained in our factual thinking about mathematical objects and about values. The transcendental consciousness has undertaken the same task—functionally identical, although ontologically interpreted differently from the Platonic myth. It relativizes factual thought and factual valuation to imperative constraints contained in the *eidos* of thought, the *eidos* of justice, and the *eidos* of beauty. It constitutes a nonrelative reality which gives us as thinkers and valuers the nonarbitrary measure of our orienteering in the world. It gives satisfaction to those who wish to have the certitude that this is how one truly thinks and truly judges.

But this satisfaction is not required in order to pursue science effectively, in order to reason effectively. The application of rules of scientific operations does not require us to know the reasons for the validity of these rules. But the knowledge of these reasons, or the conviction that we know them, is required for us to believe that that which is the outcome of scientific labors is not only useful but also true, and that there is a difference between a true explanation of the world and an explanation which is effectively applicable. The totality of knowledge as an element of our technological culture may do without this distinction. But we do not wish to be without it to the extent that we carry within us a need to refer ourselves to a mythical reality, and this need cannot be satisfied other than through the presence of myth which fixes the fundamental jurisdiction of our science in a prehistoric jurisdiction of thought as thought. It therefore fixes it in realities which precede our empirical existence as individuals, as psychological subjects, as members of a finite culture, and as particles of a finite species.

The same applies to the so-called dispute regarding the validity of induction. The criticism of a vicious circle contained in attempts at legitimizing induction through inductive procedures—Hume's criticism—has in essence remained unanswered. There is the argument that it is one thing validly to apply the rules of induction, and something else to demonstrate that validity; and therefore one can validly apply the rules of induction without a vicious circle. But to argue thus is simply to abandon validation. In fact, validation is not essential as a premise if we wish to apply the rules of inductive procedures. But it is necessary, if we are to believe that inductive operations can not only lead to effectively applicable results, but that additionally they can lead to true results.

6

Thus, truth as a value different from effective applicability is therefore a part of myth which refers the conditioned empirical realities to an unconditioned universe. It is part of the mythology of Reason, which establishes the discontinuity between Reason and the biological assimilation of the world and therefore does not wish to regard Reason as a bodily organ. If the brain is part of the body, and reason a part of the brain's behavior, epistemological valuation cannot be saved; truth cannot be saved as a quality different from technological applicability; nor can the rules of logic as a code discovered by the thinker in the nature of thought.

We need the myth of Reason to have the belief that our logic is not simply a *savoir vivre* of a community cooperating in thought, nor only a physical property of our bodily constitution or of our way of speaking. The myth of Reason is neither true nor false, since no myth falls under the dichotomy of truth and falsity. But something can be true or false thanks only to the myth of Reason.

The myth of Reason will not cease to be myth; only in deceiving blindness can it be forged into an element of knowledge. The validity of the means of proof cannot be proved before Reason's being accepted. Belief in Reason cannot have its grounds discovered by the application of Reason as such. Belief in Reason is a mythical option; it therefore lies beyond the scope of Reason. It is necessary for the self-constitution of humanity, as presence of Reason in the reasonless universe for humanity's self-identification, for a radical self-knowledge that one is something other than a plasma with more variegated sensitivity. The object of the myth of Reason is to counteract humanity's despairing acceptance of its own contingency. It is possible not to raise the question about one's own contingency, and likewise with every other ultimate question, for one can use one's life without stepping beyond immediacy. If, however, the question about human contingency appears like a hole in our thought about ourselves, then the answer which forces our acceptance of our own contingency is desperate. Those who accept human contingency, and claim that such acceptance is not desperate, do not speak the truth. The myth of Reason cleanses us of despair; it is a *ratio* against contingency but cannot itself have reasons. Yet it has behind it a right which is derived with equal arbitrariness from two options: the option for myth and the option against it.

Science is a point of view. Explaining the origins of its own legislation—logic, above all—and condemning this legislation to a contingency, it uses it in such a way that it tacitly frees it from contingency, ascribing to decisions taken in its name a not-only utilitarian meaning. Science may be conducted without the option against myth. But whenever it attempts to confirm itself in its own contingency by taking self-establishing decisions which reduce its meaning to the purely utilitarian—each time it tacitly refers to the not-only utilitarian meaning of its results—each time therefore it transcends itself. Searching for a ground for its own self-sufficiency, it no longer is self-sufficient; while opting against myth in the name of its own rules, it will not escape the vicious circle of naturalism. The endowment with meaning of the whole of knowledge cannot be validly undertaken within the enslavement created by knowledge; it also transcends these confines when the meaning given to that totality results in a break with the myth of Reason. In particular, the utilitarian understanding of truth cannot rely on empirical reasons whose meaning has just been bestowed by that understanding. It is, therefore, a valuing option against another option spellbound by the myth of Reason. Only in illusion are epistemological solutions constrained by the rigors of science, since the solution cannot without question-begging acknowledge these rigors as existing obligations whose meaning is known.

That is why scientism and naturalism are not the judgments of scientific knowledge judging the myth of Reason, but arbitrary options against an arbitrary option for myth. They do not contain a decision of Reason which judges faith; they express an act of faith aimed against faith in Reason. Whatever meaning we give to the totality of knowledge, its logical level is different from the level of every other element of that belief and also of their totality. Every element singly and all of them together tacitly contain the skeptical "No more" in relation to their own meaning, being in their content neutral and indifferent to it.

5

THE MYTHICAL SENSE OF LOVE

1

A meaning-giving illumination of the world of things is the work of myth. But the movement of our intention directed at what forms the content of myth is not understanding, or at least not mainly understanding. It is a simultaneous act of threefold surrender, which Christians have divided into a trinity which they have named the theological virtues. This threefold movement appears to pulsate with the same energy both when it is discharged in the field of the myth's gravitation and when another human being is the place of its fulfillment. It is as though a human being were able to take over that focus of radiation which awakens and frees the mythopoeic intention of love, hope, and faith; as if that which, in relation to another person, is love, hope, and faith were the specificity of undifferentiated energy directed towards mythical values. That is why we discover a mythical bond in every love, every hope, and every faith, if we are able to distinguish them from homonimic acts enclosed in conditioned realities.

2

However, the term "faith" glistens with an easily discoverable ambiguity. When we use it in order to name a conviction supported by trust or—following St Paul's intention—to name the trust itself, we notice that trust may be an act as rational as any given principle establishing the trustworthiness of anything whatever. We may endow someone with faith or trust because of his reliability so far; we trust him in the same way we trust a watch—rationally assuming it will remain within the past limits of its reliability. But personal trust is something different—precisely that sort of trust which cannot be directed towards a watch. In general, it is not a conviction but the acceptance of another person in toto, without reasons, without the need for justification or calculation. This acceptance tacitly includes a reference to another person as one who is something more than a collection of patterns of behavior subsumable under certain rules. In the empirical sense, only those behavior patterns are accepted as "given" which provide reasons for predictions; this is what is required for trust in things. But personal trust goes beyond the possibilities contained in empirical data; it is the unique experience of a person as an unique totality not bound to rationally organized perceptions; it is as if there were in us a specific power which grasps the alter ego directly in its nonempirical personal properties, its freedom, and its absolute Being. Thus, in faith we accept another person because of his mythical constitution; whereas in a scientifically trustworthy experience a personality exists only as a self-regulating collection of properties; his Being as an absolute reality is contained in the existential constitution of myth. This myth is concealed in that personal directedness which we call faith.

Thus, every faith includes the quality of myth; but conversely, all our reference to myth, even when it is not a personal reality, includes an act of faith, turning to myth as an authority thanks to which experience is intelligible. We endow it with our trust, but we seek the source of that trust not in ourselves but in that to which it turns.

Reference to myth is not knowledge, but an act of total, entrusting acceptance with no sense of need for justification. That is why, if such an acceptance is directed towards a person, it draws that person into a mythical reality. That which Jaspers calls existential communication is a participation in myth, the dwelling of persons on its territory.

3

But the same bifurcation which applies to faith also applies to hope. The term has a practical use. Here it means the degree of rationally measurable probability of the expected state of affairs or expectation with a factor of uncertainty; and in that sense it appears in probabilistic reflections and in everyday discourse.

But the energy of mythically bound hope does not direct itself towards any particular situation that is to come about. Hope is that act through which I fix the reality of my own bond with any mythical reality and am able to proceed along a road in which I believe I have discovered ruts which lead towards a meeting with that reality. Hope supports itself on a trusting acceptance which is constituted by faith, but additionally it opens up a perspective of mutual acceptance, therefore a perspective of a full and mutual acceptance of what I am and of what I turn to in assimilating myth. Thus, hope includes an experience of inadequacy and impoverishment, as well as trust in their curability.

With reference to another person hope is the place where are set in motion all those efforts through which I desire to renew an exchange of existences; I never carry this exchange through to the end, but if I desire such plenitude, I desire it through hope for which it is impossible to discover a reason. Thus, in the movement of hope, I also turn to another person as a cohabitant of the mythical field on which the exchange between us takes place. I turn to that person in expectation of healing my own incompetence, my own inadequacy, and un-self-sufficiency.

Thus, like faith, hope is present in all my reference to the world of myth; and similarly, in all hope there is present a transfer of that object, to which hope turns, into the realm of myth. For in that case, too, the other person, to the extent that he is the seat of my hope, is grasped only as a global reality, extending beyond his empirical properties; it is the absolute source and therefore unable, in mutual coexistence, to turn into a thing which it is possible to possess.

4

". . . but the greatest of these is love." Love does not have the similarly structured ambiguity of the two properties we have just described in that the term does not have a usage pointing to a state of conviction. However, there is an analogy with this same split in the distinction between the love which is the desire for material possession, and the love which gives birth to a premonition of a free unity fulfilled in giving. It is the second love which I want to discuss.

As in the case of these other qualities, the mythical sense of love is dually defined: love always contains an intention directed at a mythically constituted reality, and, conversely, all energy directed at the mythical realm carries an erotic momentum. From such a point of view, the following determinants of Eros are important: the totality of desire, the experience of origins, infallibility, the absence of rights and demands, the attempts to suspend time, and the primacy of the whole over the parts.

First, love is the hunger for a perfect overcoming of the distance in relation to what is loved, that is, a hunger for perfect unity. It therefore contains the experience of an unbearable separation, the hope of removing that separation, and the need to give oneself in total dissolution. This experience, this hope, and this need may be referred only to a mythical realm. Whatever is the focus of the love-will is always carried beyond its empirical location: God, for the mystic desiring identity with the source of Being; the idea of humanity, for the person who would like to fulfil this idea in real history; for another person, in the eyes blinded with love; even truth, for a restless mind seeking certitude. The communion which seems to wipe out the difference between *recipiens* and *receptum*, between the lover and the beloved, is consummated only in the ultimates of myth; that is, here, where reality for which the unifying sacrifice is to be consummated, appears unconditioned, and ultimate, incapable of being defined by anything other than itself. The self-aggressive, lethal energy of love is contained in it, thanks to the fact that the limit that it sets on its own movement offers an experience of the absolute.

Second, love contains the euphoric experience of originality, the experience of "Being at the beginning"; it is melted in an undifferentiated whole with the experience of a curable separation. While love lasts, it can only be a constantly renewable expectation in movement, never a sense of satiety. This is the source of incongruity in images of paradise in religious mythologies: paradise is meant to be simultaneously an experience of perfect satisfaction and of unceasing love; it has to be a square circle. It was Bernard of Clairvaux, I think, who said that in heaven there is only the start, the eternal start, the eternal spring. The heavenly realm thus imagined would be a paradise of love, but would not be a paradise of satiety. They exclude each other.

The experience of beginning, given in the movement of love,

is also given as premonition of absolute consummation. It therefore turns towards a mythically determined situation.

Third, there is contained in love in which reciprocity can be imagined (as it cannot be thought in the intellectual love of Spinoza's God, nor in the love of humanity), a specific kind of infallibility, of nonintellectual certitude, which goes beyond what is accessible to rational trustworthiness. What we know in love, we know not as a result of observation which has a descriptive value, but thanks to that intuition which arises only in personal exchange; and conversely, what we know thanks to that intution, we know for certain. That is why, in love relations between people, believing truly in the partner's love is almost like reciprocating love. That is why the words, "You don't love me any more," spoken with conviction, are always true. In love a factual error is merely self-deception and bad faith; so a mistake is inexcusable, or at least unjustifiable. The infallibility of empathy in a love encounter is a property carried in every encounter of two absolute, inexplicable realities present in the realm of myth.

Fourth, the trust which cocreates the movement of love is not constrained by calculation, demands, or obligations. In the reciprocity of love no one is obliged and no one has rights. Reciprocity is the gift of grace and grace cannot be either earned or demanded: one attains it freely and it is removed freely. In this quality, too, the bond of love transcends all practical communications; it transcends them because it is not a relationship between empirical persons but a meeting, in an effort of mutual exchange, of nonexchangeable and nonconditioned realities.

Fifth, love is the expectation of a consummation in which time is absent. According to Mircea Eliade's detailed interpretation, mythical realities are themselves distinguishable by the fact that whatever occurs in them is excluded from the real flow of historical time. It is not something that had occurred in a moment located in our calendars, but something that occurs always in the same primal authenticity, always the same as on the first occasion. Various religious doctrines make attempts at freezing time in mythical realities: whether when they talk about the eternal personal presence of their prophets, or when they ascribe to their rituals a meaning whereby these rituals are not supposed to be simply a memento, an image, a copy, or a reminder of a mythical event, but rather its real repetition, as with the contemporaneity of Christ and the dogma of Transubstantiation in Christian mythology. And so the consummation whose expectation is love has to be an annulment of real time—that is, a communion without recollection and without a future, in which there comes about a total absorption by the present, the exclusion of things past, an ultimate unconcern regarding the future, the absence of all affects directed to the future or the past—scruples, repentance, expectation, fear: the removal of the temporal vector from the experience of the world. The descriptions of mystical experience unceasingly carry that element together with a certain nihilism, which *unio mystica* produces in relation to all obligations tied with being in the world and noticeable principally among quietists. But in carnal and earthly love we seemingly discover a copy of that same exclusion of time: a complete identification with the experienced present, a total absorption in what currently is, and the absence of what is past and what is expected in experience. Fulfilled love appears to be removed from the real flow of time which is marked at each moment by memory and expectation, that is, by such properties of experience where reality is mediated; for in fulfilled love the mediation disappears. Mystics used to call the transcendence of time the fulfillment of eternity in time; but in every love it is present as a possibility. It is not, therefore, an experiential event lawfully possible in the description of the world, because in such experience time either is homogenous or is organized homogenously.

Even in a certain ruthlessness in its relation to the rest of the world or in the cruelty which the passion of love so often carries within itself, we discover a trace of that all-excluding absorption, of that ultimate immediacy which distinguishes our bonds with mythical realities.

Sixth, the loving adoration covers everything in the adored. It does not, therefore, move from part to whole; rather it transfers the perfection of the whole to each part. In both theopatic and physical passion we again find the same structure. If the divinity is the object of adoration, everything that springs from it must be adored; theodicies are clumsy attempts at rationalizing this desire to find expression for the inevitably holistic character of love; but, being rationalizations, they betray bad faith; for in trying to justify the divinity, they tend to forgive its weaknesses and faults, whereas love does not experience the need to forgive. Similarly, a loved human being can only be loved in everything; he is not loved on account of what he happens to be; but, conversely, it is because he is loved that everything that has made him what he is, is loved; that on each occasion he is what he is and on each occasion perfect.

This adoration which accepts everything in advance does not refer to empirical realities but to what is filled by the presence of myth.

Thus, both in hunger and in satiety, love reveals itself as a motion directed towards a mythical reality.

6

MYTH, EXISTENCE, FREEDOM

1

We need, however, to name the common reason on the strength of which an encounter which contains a mutual effort to bestow existence is an encounter in myth.

Philosophical culture has lived with a desire to discover words which would describe without ambiguity the conditionality of the world of experience—in other words, the desire verbally to illuminate Being, about which it is known that it cannot be grasped as an object and that its presence is not made up of the presence of objects.

There are three possible responses to this desire.

First, we may decide that it is unsatisfiable, since it is due to an entanglement into which the word itself falls due to a misuse of speech, due to verbal artefacts aimed at a vacuum. Thus, the very reflection upon the origins of this desire reveals its pointlessness and is enough for us to impose upon ourselves the peace of renunciation. Such a decision cocreates scientistic programs, empiricist philosophies, and life philosophies. From this standpoint *the conditioned reality is not explicable but does not require explication,* since its very conditionality is not covered by a word but only a semblance of a word.

Second, we may decide that the desire may be satisfied because there is a bond between conditioned realities and Being, for which there is a fitting word. To the extent, therefore, to which Being reveals itself in conditioned realities, it gives the word access. Between the two realms of reality there are media accessible to the mind. Among others, this decision encompasses all philosophies whose impact lies beyond it, in religious mythologies; all philosophy that expects to provide a meaningful interpretation of the existing revelation; and all philosophers, not dependent on existing mythologies, who believe that Being can be named: Parmenides, Spinoza, and Hegel. From this point of view *the conditioned world demands explanation and is explicable.* Finally, we may decide that the desire we are discussing reveals the imperative of a reflective spirit when its intuitions discover the non-self-sufficiency of the object, the non-self-understanding of experience; but that each naming of that non-self-sufficiency, non-self-understanding, and relativity—let alone the naming of that which is self-sufficient and non-relative—is a mistake, since words imprison things in conditionality. Nagardjuna, Plotinus, Pseudo-Dionysius, Pascal, Kant, Jaspers, Wittgenstein, and Merleau-Ponty describe this decision in various ways. In this decision *the conditioned world urgently demands explanation and is inexplicable.* The operation of explanation does not transcend that which is conditioned.

In the mad speculations of Nagardjuna who, commenting on the words of the Buddha, declares that nothing can be said about the world, neither whether it is or it is not, nor whether it is and is not at the same time, nor that it neither is nor is not;

in the labors of Plotinus who describes the One and Being and constantly negates the names he has given—even of the One and of Being;

in the negative theology of Pseudo-Dionysius;

in the uncertainties of Pascal who says it is incomprehensible that God should be and incomprehensible that He should not be; that the soul should be united with the body and that we should have no soul; that the world should have been created and that it should not have been created;

in the dry negations of Kant's *Dialectic of Pure Reason;*

in Jaspers's reflections on the organic impossibility of a positive description which would reach that which is all-encompassing;

in Wittgenstein's abandoning all attempts at verbal leaps beyond the contingency of the concrete;

in Merleau-Ponty's reflections on the incorrigible character of perception—everywhere we find the same effort, the same desire, to express the unsatisfied sense of a mystery, given that its mysteriousness cannot be cured.

In fact, the origin of the verdict, according to which the world demands explanation and is inexplicable, appears simple. It springs from a reflection upon a usage of the word "is" which is different from that which refers objects to abstract classes. Since—to recall an earlier reflection—the meaning of the empirical usage of "is" is always identified with the meaning "Is such and such," or "Belongs to such and such class," empirical usage never gives an account of what "to be" means but only of what belongs to which class. Nothing more is required in the manipulation of things and their technologically useful knowledge. However, the question, "What is it "to be" in an unconditioned sense?" cannot be withdrawn once it has been raised. We do not have an intuition of existence in the unconditioned sense of the word but only a desire for this intuition. The question therefore multiplies numerous negative answers. For it is clear that it is impossible to say of an object that it "is" in an unconditioned sense, but only that it is an element of a certain class, that is, that it is such and such.

Thus, philosophers were convinced that if the word "is" could not be understood in an unconditioned sense, then also that which is could not be referred to anything as to its condition in any respect whatever. From this they concluded that that which is, is the Absolute; since it is, it does not become, since in the intuition of becoming, that which becomes, becomes comprehensible through a comparison of what it was with what it is; whatever becomes, is not, because it is only in that sense that it is something, namely, that it belongs to a collection of its own phases. To be, therefore, was to be removed from time and change. In the frozen self-equality existence can only be expressed in the monotonous formula: "Being is," which draws the suspicion of being tautologous.

But even Parmenides, the initiator of this area of reflection, did not confine himself to this formula. He considered that that which is must be thought, since it cannot be a part of the physical world, nor the totality of these parts. Spinoza and Hegel had explained, each in his own way, why it must be so. None of them, however, succeeded in explaining what was meant by "thought" in this identification.

The puzzling expressions concerning existence may of course

be declared a fantasy and the Leibnizian and Heideggerian question, "Why is there something rather than nothing?", empty. Such a verdict will, however, always be judged a barren escape or an arbitrary surrender by all those who know that (if one may so express it) the very Being of the world may be an object of wonder, that existence need not be at all marked by that self-explanatory familiarity, but may demand a separate act of understanding which necessarily evokes its negation: nothingness. At the same time, attempts at verbal constructions which aim at awakening a transparent intuition of the act of existence never quieten the anxiety. If Gilson thinks that to this end it is enough to say that there is a difference between "having existence" and "to be existence," he is simply repeating the Christian differentiation between necessary and contingent being, without illuminating our understanding of the act of existence. On the other hand, those who assure us that they have mastered this understanding, but are unable to express it in words, are only expressing their own sense of satisfaction, an experience which, we can all assume, sprang from imagination.

In the annals of philosophy the hope of mental control of the Absolute recurs in the euphorias of fearless reason and dies in melancholy skepticism. But the questioning situation is not eliminated. We have the conviction that the words "to be" in the unconditioned sense refer to something, and that at the same time attempts at a clear and nontautological explications of the sense of these words return inevitably to various qualitative descriptions, which end up describing membership of a class and never reach the sought reality.

In other words, we have the conviction that words have their meaning-possibilities limited to conditioned realities and that an understanding of that conditionality cannot initiate the effort which would fulfill itself in its verbal designation. That which is unconditioned denies speech-control over itself. That which transcends the universe of objects also transcends the potentialities of speech and cannot therefore enter within the horizon of a scientifically valid communication but rests within the property of myth. In the face of the conviction that the extent of transmittable experience is not self-explanatory and gives no reasons for its self-sufficiency, the myth of the unexpressed, unconditioned Being cannot be bypassed.

2

Now, this "Quality of the Absolute," assuming that this expression is legitimate, is also revealed in human existence whenever we refer to it (other than as an empirical object) as free. And we do refer, at least implicitly, to another person as a free being in all personal situations: in trust, in love, in hate, in the bitterness of refusal and the disaster of parting, in the risk of fascination, in submission of rapture, and in the pangs of disenchantment. For everywhere there we are pursued by a conviction, free of doubt, that other human beings are the proper source of their being as they are, as they reveal themselves; and that they are such in precisely the same sense in which we experience ourselves to be the source of our own properties.

Now, this description of oneself is not transmittable as a valid description. Similarly, the freedom of another is not a fact which is conclusively derivable from any valid description. Every search for freedom within the boundaries of experience recognized as valuable for a description of the world must, according to Jaspers, deny freedom, while that which appears as freedom must be taken as a negative element of knowledge, a temporary gap in explanation. Given that the gaps in what we regard as explanation of human behavior are gradually filled up, there are no reasons for claiming that there is in us some gap which it is in principle impossible to fill or that there is some irreducible "residue." In any event, thought which is steered by scientific rigors finds it difficult to accept as a hypothesis the conception of a gap thus distinguished. That is why the freedom of another cannot be an hypothesis, much less an assertion. It is an element of myth, inevitably contained in our references to another as a person.

Now, a free being is an absolute. It means that it has a power of initiating, which does not allow any questions or explanations, at least in relation to certain of its revelations that others have accessible in experience. (There are as many absolutes as there are human entities; for that reason monistic philosophical doctrines cannot tolerate freedom if they do not wish to sacrifice internal coherence, so they invalidate or render powerless any experience of freedom.) This origination is infinitely full; freedom has no degrees within the bounds of its presence (no one claims that it is present in all our revealed behavior); it is therefore either boundless or it is not at all. If it is, it does not differ in any way from the freedom with which, according to Christian myth, God called the universe to life by the power of a free fiat. So the difference between a divine and a human fiat comes down to the degree of control over objects. Hence, it would be a difference between omnipotence and limited power, but not between the more and the less free, because in absolute origination there is no gradation. Freedom does not increase my power over states of affairs, nor does it diminish in states of affairs in which my powerlessness is (for instance) for physical reasons complete. Therefore, if it is beyond the horizon of scientific thought, the presence of freedom is also insignificant from the perspective of a technological attitude to the world. It is an irreducible element of our communion as persons.

Thus, in our being between things and people, the need to move towards the Absolute appears in two ways, a need which on both sides is blocked by the limitations of language. The intuition of the conditionality of experience awakens the intuition of the boundary whose impossible crossing would have led us to a non-conditioned reality; the intuition of the Other opens up a passage—which is inaccessible to rationalization—towards the absolute of someone else's freedom, present in the empirical human subject, yet different from it.

When we position ourselves in this dual contact with the mythical realms of Being—of a nonconditioned reality transcending the object and of freedom transcending the empirical subject—the act of such a positioning has no reasons which would have raised the probability (in the scientific sense of the word) of both these realms above zero level. The mythical project is deceptive if it seeks tools which are to turn it into a conclusion drawn from a record of experienced events, a record admissible within the intellectual human community in our culture. A mythical project can have no reasons, it only has motives. We have discussed them to some extent. We can clarify those which apply specifically to the mythical unconditionalities we have just considered.

3

In fact, if our empirical surroundings, the stream of coming-to-be and perishing of qualities, are self-sufficient and not related to

Being which preserves the nontemporal foundation of temporality, the understanding of the world as the coming-to-be and perishing of values is an impossibility. It is, therefore, also impossible that there should be constituted within us a self-knowledge of humanity with its discontinuity in relation to its prehuman roots, the self-knowledge of humanity as value. For the value of the concrete is acceptable only when value precedes everything concrete, when it is, before it is embodied. But Being, transcending an object, is the condition of the existence of values which precede their own embodiment. And yet human culture demands solidarity in values which appear underivable from the prehuman conditions of man, from his materiality, from his position in the genealogical tree of animate nature. Acquaintance with the pre-cultural genesis of culture cannot suffice for our participation in the community of culture; this community demands that it be referred to nonconditioned values as a point of confrontation and it is under this condition that it preserves itself. Humanity as a commonwealth is intentionally connected with transcendental conditions of experience.

But the same can be said of humanity as persons. If human personality is capable of complete integration into genetic Being, if an individual is a sperm bank, if he is just as contingent in relation to the species as the species is contingent in relation to nature (and if nature itself carries within itself the same contingency as any existential fact)—we are not entitled to assert that the autotelic meaning of personality, noted in the Kantian imperative, is anything other than a whim of a contingent culture, or could not, as a consequence of an equally valid whim, cede its place to its antithesis. If personality is not an absolute (that is, freedom), its claim upon autotelic value is thereby not just constricted but rather annulled totally.

These, I repeat, are motives, not reasons. Myth has no reasons. It does not require them, but not because it cannot have them; on the contrary—it cannot have them because it does not need them. For our reference to myth is not a search for information but a self-positioning in relation to the area which is experienced in such a way that it is a condition (not logical, but existential) of our clinging to the world and to human community as a field where values grow and wither.

4

One can say: such an argument may justify any comforting metaphysics that robs man of his dignity and provides him with an illusory rest instead of enabling him to carry on his life in the face of a reasonless world. To which I reply: such an argument contains neither a factual nor a potential justification of any metaphysic, but only an assumption regarding the hopeless impossibility of metaphysics if it consists in searching for a rationale for myth. (The assumption concerns the inability of myth to arise out of reasons; the need for reasons as such arises and is applicable within the bounds of experience.) In turn, the decision that the dignity of humanity contains the ability to support life plunged in the Unreason of the world is a noble decision but a decision in the realm of myth. However it is defined in its contents, the moment it is acknowledged the dignity of humanity inevitably transcends experience. If people declare that dignity means a life in truth, and truth is the world's Unreason, they doubly reach to the mythical basis of their own existence. They know, that is, what is dignity and they know what is truth. But they know neither the one nor the other if they do not transcend experience. The idea of human dignity, as we discussed it, transcends the totality of factual and historical humanity. The idea of Unreason as a truth about the world is inexpressible, in the sense which the quoted sayings give it, without a previous assumption of a truth which violates experience, since the interpretation of the results of experience as truth cannot spring from an accumulation of experiences.

The ubiquity of myth therefore reveals itself in the inevitable drawing from its reserves even in those acts which make a virtue of rejecting myths.

But someone will say: even if it is thus, if the binding of human consciousness with an acceptance of Unreason of Being cannot exclude a mythopoeic decision, then in any event the spirit of courage lives on the side of those who reject the myth of Logodicea in favor of the myth of the absurd. This is also the case when we acknowledge that neither myth can turn into a beneficial metaphysical truth, but that both—in acceptance and rejection— remain outside the area of the known, outside the area where one can choose between truth and falsehood. Following the same objection, the genius of bravery will remain with the myth of

Unreason whereas the fear of despair, the flight from doubt, and the search for security from the absurd, from contingency, from death and suffering, will lurk in the myth of Reason.

To this I reply: this can happen and does happen, and even happens most frequently. It can be thus, but it need not be thus. The myth of Reason, the myth of the noncontingency of the world may equally take root in the need for human solidarity, in the experience of community, and the possibility of human brotherhood; and for an understanding of this experience, for a satisfaction of this demand, and for a faith in this possibility, the myth of Reason is also indispensable. Whether the myth arises precisely from this basis, or rather from fear and the need for personal security—it is almost impossible to prove in any particular case where the mythopoeic act occurs. So, whether it conceals the mean-mindedness of an escape from despair, the bad faith of the fearful, or rather the desire of the community and a hope of a fulfilled humanity, depends each time upon the individual consciousness which performs the mythopoeic act. Only the individuals concerned can, in relation to themselves, establish with certainty whether their myths are born from the energy of fear or from a diffusion of love. One needs, therefore, a fearless radicalism of self-knowledge approaching a self-transparency; one needs the courage to unveil endlessly one's own motivation, the quality of one's own point of motion, in order to know whether the myth of Reason, given that it has been accepted, carries within itself the terror of the absurd, or a momentum of a sense of human community—or maybe both.

But someone will now say: even if it is so, the myth of Unreason is the more dignified if only, precisely, because it does not contain such an ambiguity and cannot therefore be a work of fear, it will always be a tearing of the curtain which separates us from the dark contingency of Being. It is therefore preferable, because the spirit of courage dwells in it always.

To which I will reply that it is not so at all. The myth of Unreason may surface in courage through an attempt to stand up to contingent Being; but it may be conceived in that same heaviness of fear of the ultimate question, in that same, never fully conscious, never radicalized intention to flee, which gives birth to the myth of Reason in its variants of anxiety. It may simply be a wish to identify with each succeeding given situation, with each encountered circumstance; it can be a flight from transcendence beyond immediacy. Thus, if the myth of Reason carries a fear of the absurd, the myth of Unreason carries a fear of the questioning situation as such which places us in the face of the contingent world.

That is why each mythopoeic decision may contain a rotting root of fear, but each may also be injected onto a flowering trunk of a consciousness radical towards itself. That is why the spirit of courage is not a one-sided ally of one of the two myths in conflict but can be the ally of both.

MYTH AND THE CONTINGENCY
OF NATURE

1

Thought is habitually "structuralist," if one can be allowed to employ an overworked term which has therefore become almost useless. It means that our understanding of anything whatever rests exclusively on the pairs of opposites of which the understood quality happens to be an element. In other words, we understand only through contrast, only when we can comprehend that which is the absence of the comprehended: an object can appear only against a background of a universe which it is not. The act of recognition or identification of things is simultaneous with the movement of thought which reaches what the object being recognized is not: *Omnis determinatio est negatio.* In saying that something is such-and-such, we know what we are saying only when we know that some other thing is what this thing is not. Hence, all naming which aspires to describe the properties of "everything"—for instance, "The world of experience" or "the whole of what is known"—either has only an illusory meaning, or immediately evokes the counterelement of that "all" which creates a contrast for it in a paired opposition. Thus, in the act of recognition there is an inertia which, in the face of questions regarding "everything," immediately calls up a second universe that gives a meaning to "all." "All" thereby ceases to be all, but itself in turn becomes a condition of an understanding of that second universe—hence, the birth of the Myth of the Cave or similarly shaped structures, thanks to which the whole of the experienced universe may be taken as a reflex, a sign, an appearance, or a veil of another universe. They support each other, for the hyperexistence of Platonic Ideas is only comprehensible in relation to the impermanence of palpable entities—and not just the other way round. And we are assured by Christian philosophers that the Christian God is accessible to mind not in the hiddenness of His essence but through His link with the wretchedness of creation, which He has endowed with existence only as a creator revealed in His works, never in secret loneliness. Thus, the incurable negativity of every act of recognition inevitably leads the mind to reach for myth when it wishes to name the world in its wholeness, and it avoids myth only in bad faith or in an illusion of understanding.

2

The diffusion of knowledge about just such a structuring of the act of thought has caused modern psychological, sociological, and philosophical reflection on man to abandon the hope that we should ever be able to describe the result of man's contact with Being by taking as a point of departure both these realities separately and examining in turn the share each one has in the results of this contact. Subject and object, man and culture, the ego and the world, the laborer and things—all these appear as bound pairs, of which each element is known only indirectly in relation to the state of cognition, reflection, perception, and work, respectively. In this case at least, the long-maturing philosophical reflection has become articulated in the form of an almost universally held conviction. There is the intentional structuring of consciousness and there is a situational codesignation of the object in relation to consciousness; to reach that which is truly, ultimately "given" without mediation has proved as futile as the desire to see one's own eye without a mirror. The critique of the *cogito* and the critique of all theories appealing to the ultimate given of consciousness were links in that mental labor which brought about the belief that the relation is prior to objects, that objects are points which fill up the relational net, constituted in the binding of consciousness and the world, but that within the range of the perceptual material it is impossible to separate out the share of both the elements which demarcate the perceptual situation (that at best one can only separate out its subjective deforming contribution). In the situational imprisonment of perception, a presituational consciousness, a pure receptive *potentia* is as much a speculative construct as is a pure transmitting *potentia* in the shape of the world.

The outcome of such retrenchment is to strike out from the register of permissible questions all questions regarding absolute genesis, the unconditionally original state of anything, the primacy of whatever property, since each is known only in an oppositional entanglement. All such questions turn out to be variants of the chicken and egg problem.

But we can at least focus our attention on the problem: why is the question about the chicken and the egg absurd? It may be undecidable with the help of any reconstructional hypothesis; it is perhaps scientifically useless, but it is not unintelligible. Each answer may transcend imaginable experience, but the answers are not negligible. It is doubtless negligible in the case of the chicken's egg; it is significant, however, when it concerns the "Egg of Being," so to speak. The prehuman genealogy of humanity and the prenatural genealogy of nature lie beyond the valid limits of the spheres of inquiry. But as expressing a mythological curiosity they are inescapable.

3

Assuming a situational, paradoxical character of all possible absolutes (that is, assuming that the situation of consciousness in the world is always the inescapable point, in relation to which consciousness and the world are secondary profiles cut out of a raw material categorically different from either of them as commonly imagined), then questions which are directed at them are bereft of sense; both consciousness and the world turn into nothingness from which they may be redeemed only through a mythopoeic decision. Now, this primal amalgam, from which both human and natural existence is then to take shape as differentiated constructs, does not, just by being named by us, thereby become comprehensible. The inertia of thought returns constantly, as if to a natural spot, either to humanity upon which Being is sustained, or to Being upon which humanity is fixed. No one has consistently succeeded in not splitting the primary phenomenon; for it is easy to say that we discover consciousness and Being only in the secondary apocritical operation, while it is much more difficult to discover a reason for such an operation or to describe it. Whenever we wish to offer such reason, or undertake such a description, we return to the prereflective habitual constructs of common knowledge, forgetting that philosophically we have acknowledged them as the derivatives of a primary experience. We talk of experience as if it were formless clay from which we form molds at will; but we are unable to explain how it is that, while still nonexistent, "I" should mold myself out of this clay. It is enough to concentrate on this reconstructional project in order to realize its absurdity. On the other hand, the critique of all moves which attempt to catch the cleansed "I" (that is, philosophically to cancel the Being) or the Being which we can get to know apart from the fact that it is being known (that is, to annihilate consciousness and reduce it to a sheer transparency in relation to Being) has all reasons on its side. That is why, in all inquiries regarding the ultimate stuff of the given, not only all reductions—whether realist or subjectivist—are barren; but equally barren is the naming of this stuff which ends in a desperate incoherence.

4

Hume's genius and the splendid momentum of his ascetic labors appear to depend on an understanding of this situation. His tenacious destructive critique has revealed the only world that can emerge from an attempt at a total negation of myth. It is a world condemned not to become a world truly, a world incurably filled with the ad hoc singularity of contingent fact, beyond which language and inductive thought do indeed lead us but lead us without reason. An antimythical project which is careful to retain its coherence cannot transcend Hume's vision. And in this view, every thought which runs beyond consciousness of present perception regarding whose not-perceived properties it is impossible to inquire (for instance, whether it is "the phenomenon of a lived experience" or rather "the lived experience of things")—every thought expressed in a universal judgment probably does have motives, but has no reasons. We have to remember that fire burns, since forgetfulness would be the source of pain; but we have no right to believe that fire burns. Thought is the instrument of escape from suffering; it is therefore irreplaceable to the extent that it is effective. All its other meanings are an arbitrary decision, are therefore mythical. We cannot ask "what does experience consist of?" and, similarly, "why do certain connections recur"? Thought which remains in the service of an escape from discomfort and suffering has no other support. A single fact exhausts itself in itself and does not refer to anything else; grouping facts into regularities and laws does not multiply knowledge; it produces the instruments of a more efficient manipulation of things, but it does not produce understanding or even information. Meaning does not transcend the boundaries of perceptual actuality. Thought emancipated from myth is affected with an irreversible paralysis as regards meaning, though not as regards utility or application.

On the other hand, such a decision, which drains the non-utilitarian meaning from knowledge, may itself be examined about its reasons. After all, the elements of experience, neutralized as regards their existential properties (that is, their relationship to things in themselves, to self-identical consciousness, or, finally, to each other) and brought to a self-sufficient plenitude of contingency, are not the elements of the world in the current prereflective sense. What principle then can reveal the error in common thinking? When we pose this question, it appears that in fact it is not the case that experience defines the acceptable sense for scientific thought; but, on the contrary, that science in the accepted meaning of the word demarcates what we regard as experience in Hume's project.

We constantly return to the same circular proof: every project of cleansing the data of derivative (brought about by thinking) ingredients is an epistemological utopia of philosophical radicals, if it assumes that it can do without criteria distinguishing those pure data (criteria fabricated in intellectual thought), or that the project will succeed through a return to a paradisal freshness of spiritual babyhood. In turn, the criteria are tacitly borrowed from the existing outfit of current science which, because of its socially demarcated tasks, judges certain elements of the data as useful or useless. That which is useful, which can be digested, or used as building material, deserves to be called valid experience. Spontaneous interpretations of common consciousness clearly contain useless parts. It was Hume's and his successors' achievement to identify them. They were tightening up the boundaries of immediate data, pretending that they were submitting freely to the undulations of assumption-free perceptions in order to discover what in science can be reduced to perception. In fact, they were doing the reverse: they were relying on norms present in an already constituted science; but these norms were capable of guaranteeing to all scientific work that effectiveness for which human communal life had created science as their tool, as a lengthened hand multiplied and enhanced. Thus, the social value imposed on knowledge defined the philosophical effort aimed at designating the purified experience; its extension is the pathos of scientific asceticism and the arrogance of scientific neutrality.

It is therefore clear that experience steered by such an intention cannot validate either an unrepeatable experience or the meaning ascribed by popular consciousness to all experience, if that meaning is nonoperative, that is, barren for scientific exploitation. According to these norms I cannot, for example, acknowledge my *hic et nunc* experience of another person in his suffering, love, or fear, and all my certitude and palpability of this experience is useless and pretentious. I cannot experience the world in terms of growth or diminution of values. The legislative authority which issues these prohibitions is experience given as an unconstructed element, given simply like a flowing river. In reality, however, it is a derivative authority, projected by scientific knowledge as an organ of life. But if life demands other organs, then it is within its rights; and if these organs do not require and even do not tolerate such manipulations, they are within their rights too. They therefore have the right to validate an experience which is invalid, one which, from the perspective of the constitution of the sciences, is not an experience at all. They are entitled to accept the experience of a mystic. They have a right to be concerned regarding the whole area of anxiety which is awakened by inquiries about Being and Nothingness. We are thus reiterating an observation we have already recorded: when a cleansed experience collides with myth, it is not a case of reason against prejudice, but of value against value.

5

In particular, on account of the experience defined by the constitution of science, I am unable to accept the principle of Sufficient

Reason. In the Leibnizian sense, this principle is neither an analytical rule of logic nor a report of experience. It is a postulate which endows the mythical project with a pseudo-logical articulate form. Commentators on Leibniz often identify the principle of Sufficient Reason ("In relation to every event and every truth there is an answer to the question: Why?") with the theory of universal final causation or with a description of the world where efficient and final causation merge (or, according to Schopenhauer's critique, fall victims of a confusion). But this is not a precise explanation. It would compel us to claim that Leibniz initially assumed that the world is purposefully steered in all the details of its mutations, and that he then hid the arbitrariness of this assumption in a rule which demands that this purposefulness be treated as an outcome of the irrepressible force of logic. In reality his assumption is different. He does not proclaim that whatever occurs has a purpose, but that the existence of the world is the outcome of a choice between existence and nonexistence. His reasoning is as follows: one can explain every contingent event through other events, each of which is contingent, and they are contingent as a totality; no empirical inquiry is capable of removing contingency. But acceptance of the contingency of each event separately and of their totality ends in acceptance of the contingency of the existence of the world. But this acceptance is prohibited because existence is *more difficult* than nonexistence. The question "why is there something rather than nothing?" is therefore, according to Leibniz, sensible and inevitable, and an answer to it annuls the contingency of individual events. Thus, in order to validate the principle of Sufficient Reason, one has to accept that the existence of the world is the outcome of choice, since nonexistence is *easier*.

Leibniz's doctrine seems to fail, therefore, not because it confuses two variants of causality, but because of the arbitrariness of his assumption regarding the relative position of Being and Nonbeing. Transmittable experience will never discover this observation, since it has no intuition of Nonbeing, and therefore has no intuition of existence in an unconditioned sense. Therefore the claim that Nonbeing is easier than Being (that is, more easily imaginable? always endowed with a positive presumption? or given to consciousness as an originating idea so long as proofs for existence are lacking?) also escapes comprehension permissible within the sphere of scientific rules. In this sphere even contingency as a quality of Being is inexpressible, since contingency may appear only as a relative negative quality (an event is contingent in respect to other events and therefore independent of them); it is impossible to call the world contingent, but consequently it cannot also be called necessary. The world is what it is —it does not refer to anything, it does not demand questions regarding reasons. When we call existence "contingent" (as Sartre does), we also make it clear that we have a good intuition of what the absence of Being is, the intuition of Nothingness. We then assume, contrary to Leibniz, that existence is not the outcome of choice between existence and nonexistence and that Nothingness is not at all easier than Being; but we do assume, agreeing with Leibniz, that Being and Nothingness are accessible to an expressible confrontation in thought. The equipotentiality of Being and Nothingness makes the belief in the contingency of the world possible but is an assumption as mythical as that regarding the inequality of Being and Nothingness.

8

THE PHENOMENON OF THE
WORLD'S INDIFFERENCE

I

The mythical project which demands a reply to the question regarding the contingency of Being does, however, possess a regenerating root in man's rudimentary reference to his own situation. It is an attempt to stand up to or to overcome the experience of one's own apartness in relation to the world.

The phenomenon of the world's indifference belongs to fundamental experiences, that is, those it is impossible to intercept as specific cases of another, more primitive need. This fact seems to me important. Admittedly, one can regard certain phenomena revealed by depth psychology as being more primitive and as illuminating the experience of indifference as their derivative; that, for instance, regressive fear—which produces a longing for a return to an embryonic situation, to the mother's protective womb, and for a complete release from life's responsibilities— awakens the experience of the world as indifferent. One could similarly conclude that the death drive, the wish for a total levelling of tensions which spring from the very fact of organic life, explains that appearance of the world as indifferent.

It seems, however, that it is the other way round. The longing for an antenatal shelter, for a partial death, which liberates from a responsible life, as well as the attempt to ensure for oneself an ultimate absence in the world, are already, both one and the other, the movement of escape from something—and this something must precede the need for shelter or the fear of existence.

What then are we running away from?

The simplest answer is that we are running away from suffering. But what is common and identical in all suffering: in physical pain, in the sense of failure in life, in the fear of a task above one's powers, in grief at the death of loved ones, in fear of one's own death, in rejected love, in humiliation, in realizing the hopelessness of ambition, in the experience of impotence, and in unbearable loneliness? What is the experience which allows us to cover all these situations and thousands of others with one word? What is this suffering which in such a variety of experiences is perceived as a single experience?

To say that we attempt to escape suffering, and that the flight as such defines the community of the experiences from which we desire to flee, is an apparent explanation through a tautology, just like the doctrine (famous for its barrenness) which proclaims that "men seek happiness." For it is indisputable that there are certain sufferings from which we think we should not escape. The utilitarian will argue here that the supposed suffering clearly causes us pleasure (or greater pleasure or lesser pain than its absence); it is therefore not suffering but an experience in which, despite an admixture of pain, the algedonic balance sheet is ultimately in profit. Enough has been written about the purely verbal character of such explanations for us not to return to this issue. (If we initially define our suffering through our flight, then the account that we are fleeing from suffering is a tautology; if, in turn, we state initially that we are fleeing from suffering, we are forced to define suffering differently, and in particular we have to cope with the experience which assures us that we are not fleeing from certain situations which, without a doubt, we experience as instances of suffering.)

That from which we flee is the experience of the world's indifference, and attempts to overcome this indifference constitute the crucial meaning of human struggle with fate, both in its everyday and its extreme form.

2

All negativities of life are explicable as manifestations of indifference.

Physical pain is a paradoxical experience in which that body which is me becomes indifferent in relation to me, bearing down upon me as if on a foreign object, forcing me into a situation of an intolerable distance in relation to myself. Incapable of freeing myself from a sense of identity with my own body, I also have it before me as a foreign reality, which may crush me through its insensitivity towards me, its inability to be friendly towards me who am that very reality. That is why in physical pain there constantly flashes an unexpressed feeling of difference between me and the body which I have ceased to control. If I were totally separate from that body, physical pain would not affect me—as would follow from Cartesian assumptions, which have not been carried by Descartes to their final conclusions. If, on the other hand, I were identical with that body, pain would equally not affect me. I could not—being free—experience my own body as an external evil. I could not live with a sense of helplessness in the face of its untamed and hostile energy. In physical pain I am abandoned by the body which I am. I cease to be it and become the experience of that body, that is, its suffering. Physical pain does not reduce me to my physiology. On the contrary, it reveals to me its possible estrangement, its unconquered sovereignty. In the sense of the split which arises in physical pain, the phenomenon of the world's indifference is the most acute, since it concerns that fragment of the world with which I normally experience the most direct intimacy. All our struggles with the misery of human flesh are attempts at a total restitution of identity of ourselves with our bodies; they all aim at removing the body's indifference towards "me"—who is different on each occasion— to familiarize them with "me" in a friendly trust, and in the end ensure a sense of perfect match. Cessation of pain is one's experience of returning to the body.

3

But everything in our environment of things and people which frustrates our efforts or causes misery, reveals the world to us as an intolerably indifferent reality. In dying and in the death of our loved ones, what is most acute is precisely that they become indifferent towards us, absorbed irrevocably in the place whence they ostentatiously demonstrate a complete lack of interest in us. This sudden loss of interest produces the unease which is felt at the sight of a corpse of a known person: an object, still being identified with a person, but incapable of a personal contact with us. Equally, the anticipation of our own death, that is, the projection of a world without our presence, reveals to us the indifference of Being and only for that reason it is difficult to bear. Since in projecting my own absence from the world I am unable to remove myself as an observer of the world in which precisely I am not, the anticipation of my own death does not reveal to me my own indifference towards the world (on the contrary, my own condensed self-interest in the world is the condition of my fear of death), but presents a world which has grown indifferent towards me, that is, is organically unable to observe my presence. The so-called Nothingness is not a place from which springs the fear of anticipated death, since we possess no intuition of nothingness— just as we have no intuition of existence—in the unconditioned sense, and just as we comprehend existence intuitively only in the form of belonging to the world, so we understand nothingness only as absence from the world. But we cannot anticipate our own absence from the world without simultaneously assuming our presence, that is, we are incapable of anticipating it in its extreme realization. Nothingness is not a dark room which I fear to enter, since an empty room where an unseen threat might lurk is the source of an intense experience of my presence in the world. Thus, it is not Nothingness that we fear, but a world grown totally indifferent, which has organically ceased to notice our imagined presence in it—that presence which is assumed in our imagined absence. It is the possible and soon inevitable darkening of Being in relation to my existence that fills me with terror, and not my own darkening in relation to the environment. In the anticipation of my own death, the world becomes a parental home which at a stroke has ceased to recognize its own child— and it is this projection of our nonrecognition by the world that endows our fear of death with a meaning. The phenomenon of the world's indifference nowhere else appears so saturated: the infinite privacy of death preceded by imagination, its self-sufficiency, and the absence of any reasons for it in the world mean that the indifference which Being shows us in this experience is manifested by the totality of Being in every respect and to an ultimate degree. The privacy of death also means that although we can—through a reference to Being, and above all to human realities—give a meaning to our consent to death or our readiness to die, we yet cannot impose meaning upon death itself. Since, therefore, the phenomenon of the world's indifference is nowhere so evident and so unsuited to concealment as in the experience of anticipated death, this anticipation initiates us better than anything else into that quality of Being which is dispersed in all negativities of life, although in diluted or fragmentary variants capable of concealment.

In fact, the fragmentariness in the experiencing of the world's indifference is only apparent and acknowledged in bad faith. It seems to us that it is always someone else—that other people are revealing their indifference to us when they are the palpable source of anything that we know as a negativity, the source of refusal, humiliation, or shame. It also seems to us that in our specific defeat some situation was beyond our power, some fragment of the world has gained superiority over us, or that we cannot cope with a particular situation. It seems to us then that the indifference flashes through our particular encounters with objects, with people, and with our own bodies; but that we have no cause to extend this shadowy flickering over the whole of Being in order to perceive it as the manifestation of a quality permanently attached to the world.

In fact, we could, without self-deception, admit the contingency and fragmentariness of the phenomenon of indifference, were it not for the experience of anticipating death. The anticipation of death discovers the phenomenon of indifference as the *quidditas* of the world, because it is precisely in it that the world as a whole, in all respects and to an extreme degree, is forced to reveal its indifference. From that moment, and on account of this privileged experience, all partial revelations of this indifference in singular negativities cannot be regarded as accidents where the property of only a certain fragment of the world is revealed, but rather as imperfect glimpses of a homogenous whole. Since we already know that the world may show us complete indifference and that it has to show it for certain, we thereby know that the fragmentary experiences of indifference lead us into the true *modus* of our relations with the world—that is, it is not this or that person who through indifference causes us suffering, that it is not some particular state of affairs that gets the better of us, but that through this person and through this state of affairs the silence of the world seemingly speaks to us its "couldn't-care-less" about our existence.

This does not mean of course that each of our experiences

reveals the world's indifference, since we all know that we live only thanks to various kinds of nonindifference in our encounters with people: thanks to solidarity, trust, love, and friendship. The phenomenon of the world's indifference, revealed as a property of the whole, does not cancel, does not call upon us to ignore or treat as illusory all variants of nonindifferent human coexistence on which we all depend. But the phenomenon of indifference, understood as the *quidditas* of the world, gives to the totality of human endeavors a common purpose: the constant battle against indifference.

4

We strive to overcome the indifference of the world by a technological appropriation of objects, thanks to which they become obedient to us. The satisfaction experienced through this obedience is due to the fact that to an ever-increasing extent we inhabit an environment which we have organized ourselves, so to an ever-increasing extent we feel free to ascribe to ourselves divinelike creative talents. The world had ceased to be raw nature, crushing in its insensitivity; it has almost become the emanation of our projects; vast areas of it, which constantly grow in extent, listen to our commands; it has become sensitive to our wishes. We cherish the hope that this sensitivity will grow, and we draw up dizzy plans of a technological empire subject to our orders. If the world were the work of divine free will, it could not remain indifferent towards the divinity; and in submission to divine omnipotence it would have to demonstrate humility, gratitude, and worship of the creator. We too imagine that, depending on the extent to which we are able to achieve the status of a collective divinity in our imagination and the extent to which we force upon things the gradual decrease of their incalculable intractability, so, appropriately to the level of obedience which things show us, the world turns into a domestic animal; the boundary between the efficiency of a machine and the friendly trust of a tamed animal begins to blur. Technological triumphs offer us the physical world fully humbled.

But all our successes in controlling things are constantly accompanied by worries of unfulfillment. Technological culture enables us to grasp the world as booty but it cannot abide its indifference; the taming of things is only apparent, the sense of an encounter with nature in reciprocity is illusory, like the love of a necrophiliac. Nature is obedient not in reciprocity but precisely through its indifference. A world saturated with traces of our technological activities, and therefore a world seemingly human-ized, stamped in every detail with the intensity of our interven-tions, again begins to appear a nightmare. Why do we carefully preserve enclaves of natural growth between the lanes of our motorways; why should we be concerned to preserve from anni-hilation the remnants of vanishing flora and fauna and to guard wild mountains against erosion; why in fact do we experience nostalgia for the primitive (or rather, the more primitive) mate-rial environment; why the grotesque mass escapes into nature? Already we regard as natural objects refined by man, though less refined than some other objects, yet closer to their original state found in nature. In the face of a remorseless expansion of artificial materials, traditional ones—metal, wood, glass, leather, wool, and clay—appear to us friendly in their naturalness when we confront them with objects whose provenance we are unable to guess by touch, in which technological refinement had erased all traces of the raw material. What is the real meaning of the hope-less complaints over the dehumanized machine era, which should surely be regarded as an era of the humanized object? Whence the fear of a world of robots, whence the visions of man humiliated by his own automata? What kind of strange reversal leads us to perceive a snow-covered forest or a mountain stream as suddenly a more human sight than the automatized factory?

Ultimately, the attempted technological coercion aimed at pulling the material world out of its indifference ends in defeat; not because it is impossible to control infinite nature absolutely, but because at every stage of technological success things are our booty and not the fruit of a friendly fraternization; we arrogate them, knowing that they obey us because they do not signify anything, and have no meaning antedating our interventions. We are unable, therefore, to achieve that intimacy with the material world in which the alchemists believed when they understood that world as a system of signs revealing through their meaningful qualities, an entry into a secret reality which is different, truer, and not accessible directly. What is more, the paradoxical experi-ence, whereby portions of the world untouched by man begin to

seem more human than others which have been perfectly prepared for our use, is not surprising. For we are not afraid that,
literally, sometime in the future (as sinister negative utopias
sometimes persuade us), machines will, without human participation, revolt against us. Such fantasies are only an aberrant
expression of a dim premonition that a world fully mastered by
technology appears alien to us precisely because its behavior becomes fully predictable. A world of things which are completely
natural appears to us alien and indifferent because it comes up
with surprises in which we can detect neither friendship nor
hostility. On the other hand, perfect predictability is a property
which is distinctly different from what we know of relations
between people, above all in personal relationships. In encounters with people, in which we succeed in loosening the rules of
thing-like exchange, and give vent to the spontaneity which pul-
sates on both sides, we find that our inability to predict, and
indeed its uselessness, is a specifically human value. Interpersonal
calculation is instead a characteristic of practical ties between
people: all spontaneity is creative and therefore transcends the
expected qualities of human ties. Thus, terrified by the unpredictability of the physical environment in which we experience its
indifference, we later discover, as we conquer its whims, the same
or even a more acute indifference in a world reduced to complete
predictability, in a world of things that we can harness but never
domesticate. The unknown world may be a source of terror, but
so can a world only too familiar, whose course is well known
because we ourselves have charted it. Our laments over a dehumanized planet filled with machines, our miserable flights into
shrinking preserves of wilderness, are an expression of the defeat
suffered by the metaphysical project hidden in the technological
expansion of humanity—the project of domesticating matter.
The trap laid by the Unreason of physical Being has crushed us:
the indifferent world over which we once had practically no control, an unpredictable world full of puzzles and whims, was the
world which we were capable of domesticating through a mythical understanding, ascribing to its excesses a meaning not directly
perceived—the hostility or graciousness of another being which
spoke to us through a code of nature. In things subordinated by
us (thanks to centuries of dramatic technological labors) we are
no longer capable of discovering a mythical order and of taking it

seriously. Just because they are harnessed onto a wagon we are able to steer, physical energies appear to us overwhelmingly more dehumanized, more indifferent, fully nonsensical, although we have sensibly included them in our projects. We long for the unpredictability of things, for an irreversibly lost paradise of the wild. We have been longing for it since the eighteenth century, from the first moment when mechanized industry began to change the surface of the earth. It took a world of things organized by ourselves to demonstrate to us its indifference from which we aimed to escape through that organization. Having lost our ability to return to a mythical understanding of material Being, we have lost hope of domesticating and humanizing it. We stand facing objects which obey us just because they are infinitely indifferent to us.

5

There is another way in which we attempt to overcome the indifference of the world: through a desire to possess objects. The aim of the ownership relationship is for objects to lose their undifferentiated character through an exclusive unambiguous subordination, and to be filled with the same sense of non-transference which I experience in relation to myself when I imagine, or when it seems to me, that I am my own property. Surrounded by objects over which the community allows me exclusive rights, whose exclusivity related to me it is ready to defend in law, I sink into an illusion that I am experiencing an intimate understanding with my properties, that I embrace them and transpose them into a field of personal existence, where they shed their material coverings and reveal their quasi-human ability to be on intimate terms with me.

But the failure of my hope to domesticate objects through a tie of possession is worse and more degrading for me than my dissatisfaction with technological success. Technological success does not enable me to master the tongue of Being, but does create a sense of real, though partial, value in which I participate. The passion for possession means that I imagine my negative tie with other people—namely, my legal exclusivity in commanding objects—as a positive tie with the object itself, and I thus create a value out of a situation which sets me against other people. My life as a person, freely determined by that apparent intimacy with objects, thereby loses it rootedness in the human community and becomes circumscribed by the extent of my possessions. Instead of humanizing the object I possess, I surrender to a determination by the object as *mine,* that is, as snatched from others. In my satisfaction as an owner I bring about an outcome which is contrary to the one I desired: I become the sum of my possessions. This may be a trivial and oft-repeated observation, but it is worth repeating if it brings this passion into the homogenous sense of human endeavors as well. It has nothing to do with the childish morality based on a scorn for ordinary human comforts. But it has a value to the extent that in general we need a certain alertness or radicalism of memory which retains the knowledge of all the illusions of human satisfaction. I may of course slide through life in dreamy satisfaction with my possessions. But I cannot turn this life into a test of humanity, and I cannot quite rid myself of the discomfort which will lurk in the intuition (shouted down and denied) that the passion that I allowed to grip me has disinherited me from the human commonwealth, and thereby disinherited me from personal existence.

6

My attempts to overcome the indifference of the world through my communion with people need not necessarily be unsuccessful, but their success will never be complete.

In an erotic encounter, where the experience of a bond may be experienced most intensively, we perhaps reach the ultimate barrier to our efforts at pulling the world out of indifference; and we thereby convince ourselves that such a barrier really exists and, moreover, we acquire the best possible self-knowledge regarding what it is that we are after in domesticating the world.

In the intimacy of the erotic encounter we each time attempt to reinstate the reality of the ancient androgynous myth. It seems to be true—and in accordance with popular belief—that the longing of the lost half desiring again to become a part of the unhappily split whole animates our sexual interest. Seemingly tearing through the skin of our sexual partner, we attempt to possess his or her body totally, by all possible means of reception, to reach the partner in such a way as to eliminate completely all sense of difference, and to attain a shared absorption. In the asymmetry of normal sexual intercourse, the expansive male half seems to seek absorption, while the receiving female part seeks to absorb. This imbalance is noted by certain myths—which in any event have long been exploited by psychoanalytical and Bergsonizing literature—which discover a congruence of sexual satisfaction with nourishment and place it in the rudimentary stratum of life or underline the presence of the death drive in sexual desire. This same imbalance is probably confirmed by the circumstance that a fullness of sexual understanding is possible, not where it is an exchange of strictly mutual desire, but where both sides—the male and the female—concentrate the experience of communion upon the woman's body, where therefore the woman displays her surrender in concentrating attention on her own rather than her partner's body, while her partner adopts the opposite attitude.

The erotic conspiracy seems to create conditions for the illusion of complete identity, and in its tension unmasks the real sense of all our dissatisfactions, which therefore are so easily described in sexual symbolism. It reveals that the phenomenon of the world's indifference is correlated with the experience of self-identification, and that the irrevocable separation in relation to the rest of Being is contained in the very act of this self-revelation. It reveals that we experience this separation as the world's indifference, because we know that we really cannot and never will be able to transmit ourselves to any one or to anything in the quality of self-experiencing; that therefore self-identification separates us in a certain distinctive respect from everything, while all forms of communication, coexistence, help, friendship, and love, though they make our existence possible, are unable to breach this barrier of nontransmittability. The erotic communion is capable of actualizing the maximum of interpersonal communication, or even momentarily to create an illusion of identity with another, and is therefore invaluable. But the imperfection and fragility of this illusion is nevertheless constantly present in our experience. We are unable properly to satisfy a dual demand: to preserve the state of possession in relation to ourselves, and simultaneously to overcome the separatist, exclusive character of that property, that is, to compel the world to abandon its indifference towards us. The whole of mysticism is an effort to cross the boundary that is accessible in erotic communion: the effort to abandon our own ability to recognize ourselves. It betrays an inability to reconcile the two desires just mentioned because it consents to the mystic relinquishing his humanity in attaining a union with a divinity.

7

All attempts at identification with other people or groups of people (above all with irrational groups), all those efforts imitating that momentum whose limiting example is the sexual communion inevitably reveal their deceit. It may be that those eupatrids of the spirit who have experienced the bliss of mystical ecstacy are able to believe that this is not so. Flights from the indifference of the world via edifices which enable us to be absorbed in communal life through identification with family, tribal, or national groups is not by any means worthless; but it does seem that in this respect the all-or-nothing rule prevails, that therefore partial or fleeting identifications do not truly exist. The search for contact with others through the ideal of charity or attempts, in the greed for power, to arrogate people as though they were things cannot supply satisfaction either; nor do the attempts, through homoerotic love, to break the limits which sexual parity imposes upon the possibilities of understanding or of arrogating another person.

8

It is also possible to give up the attempts to overcome the indifference of the world, and this can happen in two ways. One such form of abandonment is suicide, that is, an attempt at ensuring my absence from the world and thereby annulling the indifference as a situation which seemingly also contains me necessarily; suicide therefore contains a utopian desire to pay back to the world that same measure of indifference which it had shown me, a desire to mete out a retributive punishment. This wish is ineffective and that is why suicide as an attempt to annul my relationship with the world misses the target I have in mind: the world is not punished, and its indifference does not undergo change following my absence, since it is only in my mind, not in Being itself, that the world's indifference towards me implies my presence. Indifference is not a special case of the movement of intention, but rather its absence. It is only in my mind, where it is experienced as insatiability, that indifference takes on the deceiving form of a special relationship that the world adopts towards me.

Another form of abrogation consists of a decision to accept the indifference of the world in a complete understanding and to entrench those situations of human coexistence that are accessible to us, rejecting the temptations of perfect solutions and seeking partial satisfaction; abandoning futile attempts to make the world friendly and standing up to its eternal intractability.

Such a project must awaken an elemental sympathy among all those who have set up a demystifying passion as the supreme value of their own relationship to the world. But it is not certain whether such a project is realizable. If in fact the law of all-or-nothing applies to our fundamental relationship to Being, the project of standing up to the indifference of the world in full self-knowledge is either the consent to despair or another attempt at mystification, which counts on partial solutions where global or none are the only ones possible. Since despair as a permanent state is an impossible decision, the described intention must, by force of natural movement, constantly slide towards consciousness so constituted that it will push away the constantly recurring knowledge about the intractability of the world, and will dissolve or neutralize its pressure through distraction, through entertainment, and through an apparently imposed but actually freely chosen busyness. The whole of our civilization is at the service of these apparent neutralizations by multiplying the occasions for distraction, for diluting life in the smooth flow of ritualized custom or in partial satisfactions which it is impossible to endow with universal significance.

9

In fact, the experience of the world's indifference creates the alternatives: *either* we shall overcome the alienness of things through their mythical organization *or* we shall conceal this experience from ourselves in a complex system of arrangements which distract life in daily facticity.

For it is myth, be it religious or philosophical, that has the power of removing the world's indifference, in contradistinction to all the attempts we have described, and to which we do not ascribe any meaning which transcends the empirical properties of the world: in contradistinction to a technological harnessing of objects, to attempts at appropriating another person in sexual encounter, or to the passion of possession or of power.

The flight from myth can be effective. I have in mind here those myths which do not confine themselves to explaining the partial elements of our lives or partial values through their relativization in relation to unconditional nonempirical realities, but rather those that fully gather all experience into that relativization, and therefore bring it about that empirical Being loses its own weight and begins to appear as a derivative reality, a carrier of a code transmitted by a nonempirical, unconditioned mythical world.

We postpone the question: Can the mythical project be truly assimilated so that it would forestall suspicion, stifle the alertness towards its own arbitrariness; that, in a word, it could be expressed as a kind of substance derived from a natural secretion of a spiritual system, and not as an artificially introduced nourishment?

It appears, however, that myth can in fact create a sense of the domestication of Being. As we said already, there are two extreme experiences between which our knowledge of the world's indifference is stretched: the anticipation of our own death, in which the phenomenon of indifference reveals its global character, and the experience of erotic communion, in which the attempt, pushed to an extreme, of communication with others reveals to us the presence of unbreachable barriers to the annulment of the phenomenon of indifference. Myth must give an account of both these experiences—of death and of love—if it is to perform the function under discussion. It must reply to the question: Why, in anticipating death, do I face the phenomenon of indifference as a universal property of the world? Why can't I in erotic encounter overcome the boundary which separates me from perfect union?

9

MYTH IN THE CULTURE OF ANALGESICS

1

Among the distinctive features of twentieth-century culture, especially of its present phase, we observe an apparent contrary motion of two tendencies, one of which is heard in the dominant streams of intellectual and cultural life, while the other is an attitude to life moulded by so-called mass culture.

In contrast to the bewildering restlessness of all these areas of culture—scientific and philosophical thought, as well as artistic activity stemming from the antipositivistic turning point—demonstrate a certain permanent characteristic: the conviction that man is totally responsible for the world of objects (I deliberately use the polysemic term "man"). The phenomenological analysis of the intentional structure of consciousness has turned objects into constitutive products of the very activity of consciousness. Existentialist philosophy has identified the world with successive acts of selective projection which is compelled—even if consciousness hides this compulsion from itself—to impose meaning upon objects according to a totally free choice. Those versions of Marxism which are currently most lively—in contrast to the old evolutionist versions—also aim at a view of the world from which the factor of practically oriented human intention cannot under any circumstances be removed, which therefore always has an horizon organized by human communities.

But quite independently, scientific culture also reinforces the same conviction about our irremovable presence in nonhuman realities described by science. The greatest achievements of theoretical physics in our century—the theory of relativity and the principle of indeterminacy—reach the nonprofessional communities in a form in which they appear to persuade us that the presence of an observer or an experimenter cannot be removed from a description of natural laws. Methodological reflection upon the nature of experimental knowledge (above all, the theory of operational definitions) supports the view that experimental and measuring activities must constitute an essential part of definitions, thanks to which we characterize the objects we measure and study, and that therefore it is impossible to describe an object without describing the effective activities which are necessary for its examination. It may also appear that by revealing the actual dependence, which links the states of our organisms with our conscious and unconscious experiencing of our own states, psychosomatic medicine ought to support the conviction regarding our responsibility for our own body, which can be the object of self-knowing regulative action from a purely subjective side.

Equally, in the most characteristic efforts of artistic culture—literature, music, and the plastic arts—we observe an increasing prevalence of such forms of communication in which the creator's conscious desire is to make the recipient a cocreator, who independently imposes a meaning upon the perceived work ("the open work," as Umberto Eco calls it).

Thanks to the work initiated by Marx, economic theories ceased to confine themselves to a description of a world of economic dependencies with their fateful quasinatural laws and made possible a conscious steering of productive processes and exchange at the national and multinational level.

From a world which is given in all its detail, ready-made, determined in its evolutionary process, and accessible either to description which registers its properties while minimizing human intervention, or to exploitation incapable of altering the evolutionary course of the whole—we have moved to a world which from the beginning and in every phase we have to regard as partly our own product.

We may therefore assume that our culture in all its various ramifications will popularize the sense of responsibility which each individual has for the world, for his own presence in it, and for his own situation.

In reality, the attitude to life which predominates in mass culture appears to be the exact opposite of this assumption.

Many social thinkers (to name Erich Fromm as representative) anxiously note that the cultural situation of industrially developed countries is characterized by a decisive collapse of the so-called "spirit of initiative" and of the sense of personal responsibility for oneself and one's community. This may be seen as either the decline of civilization or a natural outcome of technological progress, but as to the facts themselves there appears to be a consensus.

Undoubtedly, the technological circumstances themselves and the conditions of production and exchange associated with them may in part be taken as an explanation of this decline. Less and less do results of technological efforts depend upon the unforeseen ingenuity of brilliant individuals. The nineteenth-century inventor, whose stereotype model is Thomas Edison, is clearly on the way out. The position of a single individual's invention has been replaced by the collective labors of constructors working according to a planned division of tasks upon huge enterprises, which no one can grasp in all their detail—hence the growing anonymity of the great technological gains of this century. The inventor of the steam engine, the radio, the telephone, are known to all by name; despite the colossal growth of information, the constructors of radar, calculating machines, lasers, and satellites are either unknown to the general public or effectively cannot be known, because of the difficulty of establishing a clear distribution of achievements in the performances of large creative teams. The same phenomenon appears in science, although to a lesser extent. The eruption of a great individual initiative, to which one could give full credit for a clear achievement taken all the way to its technological or experimental phase, is necessarily less and less common.

The concentration of capital, accompanied by its growing anonymity in capitalist countries, and the planned direction of the nationalized productive organism in the socialist system, must in both instances produce analogous phenomena in our understanding of economic life. Equally, the type of entrepreneurial industrialist achieving a private fortune through his own ingenuity or iniquity—but always on his own account—is clearly a dying species. Vast accumulations of capital are less and less tied to individual names. The dominance of huge corporations in the mercantile market is also an irreversible trend. Consequently, the general and attested belief that people are capable of effectively commanding macroeconomic processes is matched by a sense of helplessness in individuals regarding their own ability to influence not only broad economic events but also their own position within the economic mechanism. The more the material world is open and full of possibilities for large human groups, the more it is an established and irremovable reality for each separate individual, the less room it offers for effective individual initiatives.

The constantly expanding division of labor and the institutionalized control over increasing areas of life lead in the same direction. Institutionalized education already covers the totality of the preparatory stage of human life from the third year to the final educational phase. At the same time, the idea initiated by socialist movements that the community is obliged to find everyone a place in the overall system of production has also gained general acceptance.

We can all observe these processes and they are generally known. Equally apparent, and not worth enumerating, are their results in diminishing human suffering and increasing the reserves of energy available to humanity. All the same, their destructive results cannot be disguised. A community which is rationally organized or which aims at rational organization gradually removes from me and from each one of us our responsibility for our own lives, for the lives of others, and for the whole community. The totality of structures in a collective life presents itself to me as a kind of a gigantic insurance system. Whatever might stimulate my feeling of responsibility is an object of professional interest for certain institutions specifically designed for that purpose, and to people employed to show that interest. I need not concern myself with the education of my own child, since there are a number of people to whom the social division of labor has entrusted this concern. I need not consider that I am responsible for the pedestrian next to me who collapses unconscious on the pavement, since I know that special social, police, or medical organizations are there to be alert to his fall, remove him from the pavement, revive him, or bury him. Other institutions take over responsibility for my marriage, my sexual life, my illness, my employment, and my death. True, I also have my own share in the social division of labor; I am obliged to perform effectively the duties associated with the position I hold. But even if I let myself go or turn to drink, there are institutions whose job it is to prevent my fall or restore my health. I can learn from popular books how to avoid or delay a heart attack or a stomach ulcer if I organize my mental life properly. But this does not mean that I am responsible for my own body. It means simply that I should consult a psychiatrist, as well as a heart specialist, and get a prescription for a more comfortable arrangement of my spiritual interior. To an extent, this is connected with the process of the disappearance of professions which, apart from being defined by special skills, were also seen as a calling. The professions of doctors, nurses, teachers, even artists, and even of soldiers, were all associated with a sense of a voluntarily undertaken mission. In our world, each profession is no more than a number of skills and knowledge which make possible the performance of tasks envisaged for specific positions in the social organism.

Someone might say: these are obviously irreversible processes and grieving over them is like wishing for the resurrection of time past. To this I reply: were I to believe that the single-track and irreversible process, which is gradually washing away each one's sense of responsibility in order to transfer it to all of us together, will inevitably dominate the coming era, I would need to believe that the end of humanity is near. In fact, the category of responsibility makes sense only to the extent that it is tied to the category of the person. In this respect I share Kierkegaard's principle: collective responsibility is a fiction if it is something other than a sum—literally a sum—of individual responsibilities. If it is only some collectivity, and only that collectivity, which is responsible in a specific sphere, but no single individual, then the weight of responsibility rests simply on the universal, that is, Nobody.

It may be that the contrary motions of the two tendencies, noted at the beginning, may be understood in the sense that the first—characteristic of philosophical and artistic attempts at taming the world—is a natural self-defense reflex against the dangers of the second tendency which takes root following the increased interdependence and higher degree of organization in life introduced by modern technology and its organizational consequences. In this sense, art and philosophy (together with the philosophical interpretation of scientific results) are the organs producing antibodies, which to an extent neutralize the destructive results of processes which force all of us to consent that we are determined totally by our place in the social fabric.

2

Among the important but little-noted aspects of our civilization is the complete departure from a belief in the value of suffering. The belief that suffering is or may be the source of value is present in most of the primitive cultures we know and is voiced in such common phenomena as the severity or even cruelty of initiation rites. The same intuition was expressed in Christian culture in all those elements which justified the need for ascetic practices, and the whole severity or even hostility in man's attitude towards his own body.

In popular secular thought regarding archaic religions, concepts which were created and diffused by evolutionism in religious studies pervade our civilization. According to these views, such rituals as initiation tests form part of a museum devoted to a teratology of culture and are usually relegated under the rubric, "The savagery of primitive peoples." These views are just a few of the innumerable reasons for the blissful sense of superiority with which we, released from barbarous superstitions, observe the dark insanities of primitive folklore. The Christian cult of suffering, ridiculed and attacked in much the same terms that were employed by Renaissance humanism, has retreated from our civilization to such an extent that even within Christianity itself it already seems either absent or meaningless. By its own behavior the Christianity of our own century bears witness so pervasively to the triumphs of its opponents. It is so fearful of Enlightenment criticism and so cowed by its strokes that it dare not, at least in open educational work, reveal many essential elements of its own traditional view of the world; and step by step it robs its inheritance of elements which are patently in conflict with industrial civilization. The model of Christianity which most evidently is entering its triumphal stage is the most extreme departure from the Gnostic, Manichean, and Neoplatonic traditions. Overwhelmingly, it attempts to suppress a vision of the world centered on the idea of original sin, the corruption of human nature, and the real existence of evil in the world. It has fully distanced itself from the Platonic contempt for the flesh. In a specially developed variant of the model, created by Teilhard de Chardin's philosophy, Christianity becomes a belief in the salvation of matter; it sanctifies all being as divine offshoots, and is quite oblivious of the areas of darkness in the world. In contrast to classical theodicies, Teilhard's philosophy does not content itself with treating evil or sin as raw material unerringly employed by God on every occasion to build a future world of the blessed; but imagines in a euphoric vision an imminent ultimate reconciliation of the temporal world with God, abandoning the supremely Christian idea of permanent conflict between what is transient and what is infinite, and drawing a paradoxical view of the world, which in its very temporality will attain the value of an Absolute.

It is true that the cult of suffering, stemming from the Neoplatonic roots of Christianity, had for centuries been an organ endlessly and shamelessly employed by Church authorities to justify harm and oppression; that it immeasurably served the privileged classes in their concern to strengthen their privileges. It is impossible to exaggerate this circumstance, but neither is it possible not to observe that day by day it is losing its force and that the model of Christianity, tailored perfectly for the use by the privileged classes, has irreversibly moved onto a position of a despairing defensiveness, and that the force of its resistance is crumbling hopelessly.

It may appear eccentric to raise the issue of the value of suffering in a world which continues to be full of torment, oppression, fear, and the nonsatisfaction of elementary needs. It may seem that this very questioning threatens a slackening of the tension necessary in man's tenacious struggles with the miseries of basic deprivations. For, after all, a cult of suffering so conceived that it turns into an indolent resignation, a cringing acceptance of one's own destitution, an assent to evil seen as inevitable and therefore surrounded with an empty halo of sublimity, is inimical to man.

But there is a difference between rejecting a masochistic cult of suffering which masks an impotence in the face of evil or sanctifies a cowardly submissiveness, and looking, in obsessive fear, for painkilling drugs which would enable us to shut out the realities of evil from our consciousness, or to drown its presence in voluntary self-intoxication.

Among the outstandingly distinguishable aspects of our civilization is a belief (practiced rather than expressed) that security from suffering is worth any price, and specifically that those goods, whose values it is impossible to measure but which are unavailable without pain, are the inventions of maniacs or a residual superstition.

Even the remarkable medical triumphs over illness and physical pain—achievements which are most unquestionable and most apparent—have for some time been associated with phenomena causing disquiet not only among philosophers and religious prophets but also among doctors themselves. The prophylactic obsession and the cure obsession bring about the commonly known phenomena over which doctors have lost control: the enormous abuse of drugs, connected with the growing loss of medical effectiveness of many of them but connected above all with side effects, which in turn demand further medical responses. These phenomena have a long documented history, but tracing them to their sources in people's attitude to life, popularized by industrialized civilization, is less common. It seems at times that the fear of illness is more severe than illness itself, and fear of pain more acute than pain. It looks as if, by multiplying artificial limbs and substitute organs for the body, our civilization has entered a blind alley: there is a constant need to discover new cures and new prostheses to combat the unintended negative results of previous applications of cures and prostheses. Above all, the misuse of analgesics, sleeping pills, and neuroleptic cures seems almost to confirm the gloomy diagnoses, propounded some decades ago by those philosophers who observed a significant characteristic of our culture in the gradual withdrawal of the biological potential of the human organism in favor of artificial substitutes. We are getting accustomed to a rhythm of life determined by successive mutual neutralizations of stimulants and tranquilizers, as if the notorious advertising slogan, "An artifical leg is better than your own!", were displaying its first triumphs in the sphere of the chemistry of the brain.

The malicious might regard these admittedly banal remarks as an attack on medicine or childish dreams about the return to nature or, to quote Gabriel Marcel, as a call to "a spontaneous trust in life." But there is nothing I find more alien than the utopia of a paradisal state of nature. We can, however, claim that the social attitude to medicine and the way its results are used cannot be explained as the automatic outcome in the evolution of medical knowledge, but are always rooted in the attitude to life specific to the given civilization, and which in its turn influences the direction of medical research. And the attitude towards medicine in industrially developed countries is a particular instance of an attitude to life which is dominated by a constant anxiety over the question: "Is the world giving me a full portion of the happiness due to me?" The obsessive fear of suffering, of failure, of the weakening in our social status, the obsessive resentment towards those who are successful, the inability to deal with misfortune and pain without assistance—all these are symptoms of the same phenomenon: the loss of our ability to face life: the loss of instruments, with whose aid an individual can (drawing on his own spiritual resources) restore his own balance in the face of disasters and sufferings and the growing dependence on a complicated system of instruments which regulate the disturbed psychic homeostasis from outside. This fear of a situation in which one has to rely on one's own strength reveals a self-doubt, a constant demand from the world for assurance, acceptance, and recognition—ultimately the creation—of my existence; a doubt whether I was in possession of such means as would enable me to endure even minor defeats. We see in this fear false attempts to overcome the world's otherness, namely, the attempt to overcome it through escape and concealment. Drugs and alcohol cooperate in this same process: instead of undertaking the burden of independently absorbing the frustrations or overcoming the problems of communications with others, we have at hand an artificial psychic environment, which either dissolves the frustrations in immediate excitations or creates an illusion of understanding, to act as cement in social relationships.

And this panic flight from suffering appears even more destructive in the sphere of interpersonal ties and psychic life than in the sphere of physical pain. When I say that we live in a culture of analgesics, I have principally in mind those organs of civilizations, those customs, and those models of communal existence, thanks to which we are able to conceal from ourselves sources of suffering without attempting either to remove them or to face them.

We flee from an anticipation of death, which is a source of suffering—but not, however, so as to come to terms with the inevitability of death, but so as to push it out of our minds, to eliminate from life confrontations with ultimate questions, to allow ourselves to be swallowed up totally in everyday immediacy. We flee from love, which is or can be a source of suffering, shackling ourselves in a forced cynicism towards the whole field of sexuality, and forced by fear to abandon those enrichments of life which in love are rarely achieved without pain.

We flee into conformity and impose it on our children, fearful of the calamities which alienation from one's milieu piles upon an individual; incapable of believing that every attempt at self-consitution by man amounts to a break with conformity, and that there is a whole world of difference between human solidarity in work and creativity, and sliding through life along ruts of foolish chatter in a benevolent atmosphere of amity which always reaches its peak when there is nothing at stake.

We flee from solitude—but not so as to overcome loneliness through an effort which mutually enriches communication with another, thanks to shared values. We become incapable of enduring solitude in whatever form; we carry transistors in our pockets so as not to be surprised even for a moment without company. Every break in the process of mutual affirmation through the presence of others seems to us threatening.

In these conditions human community is likely to disintegrate under the merest threat. Where there are no crowds, we do not bump into each other—that is all. A community which depends solely on people not bumping into each other when there is space perishes the moment it gets crowded. We expect the overcrowding to diminish constantly and therefore such a community to be sufficient; but these turn out to be fragile calculations, even when applied to demographic projections.

The culture of privileged classes has evolved various forms of good manners and drawing room *savoir-vivre,* that is, rules for not bumping into one another for people who have enough room. These rules are ineffectual in situations where there is a real clash of interests. The culture of the underprivileged classes has created forms of real fellowship and assistance—fellowship in deprivation and assistance in the face of threat. Modern civilization, without removing either a feeling of deprivation or a sense of threat, increasingly destroys a sense of fellowship among those who are experiencing deprivation and destroys the self-help abilities of those who are under a common threat. Deprivation and threat have ceased to draw people together.

The civilization of analgesics offers an apparent overcoming of loneliness and an apparent solidarity which has a negligible endurance factor. An inability to bear suffering is an inability to participate in a real human fellowship, that is, a fellowship aware of its limits, aware of all potential conflicts that it contains, and ready to set its limits to the test.

The fellowship of those watching television together, of those watching in a sports stadium, of those drinking at the same table, of those lying in the same bed—these are all undoubtedly forms of social behavior which generate communally experienced tensions. But the strength of these tensions does not extend beyond the level necessary to diffuse the hostility of those standing in the same queue, travelling in a crowded tram, waiting for an apartment, or motoring along the same highway.

The narcotization of life is an enemy of human fellowship. The more we are incapable of enduring our own suffering, the more easily we endure that of others. The harder it is for us to tolerate loneliness, the more of it we create. The more we care for distinguishing ourselves, the more imprisoned we are in conformity. We constantly wish to be at the heart of fashion, that is, we wish to achieve the perfectly average; and at the same time to draw attention to ourselves with our favorable extraordinariness. Out of these conflicting desires, which oblige us to keep up with the rhythm of change and simultaneously to emphasise the praiseworthy uniqueness of our own rhythm, springs the inevitable speeding-up of fashion. It isn't that one cannot stay in fashion long without changing, since fashion changes quickly; it is rather that fashion changes quickly because one can only be fashionable for a short while. I am truly fashionable only during an indefinable moment at a crest of a wave. A fashion which establishes itself thereby kills itself; what is commonly fashionable thereby becomes unfashionable, and truly fashionable is only what is not yet fashionable, and for only a moment before it does become fashionable. The fragility of fashion is the outcome of a self-contradicting desire which underlies the effort to be fashionable: to be perfectly unique within perfect conformity. Only the purely physical limits set on production and on the speed of information limit the mutability of fashion.

However, this paradoxical fear of losing one's ordinariness, identified with losing oneself, that desperate longing for the ordinary which is to make me extraordinary is only the most glaring manifestation of a civilization permeated with an accelerated dissolution of traditional bonds. When I regard the whole human world as my welfare system, if all my interest is contained in a ceaseless anxiety that this world is not giving me my due, if I think that it is my property as a reservoir of satisfaction, without however being one as an object of my concern—my behavior can be effective only to the extent that I am an exception in this attitude, that is, to the extent that the world as a whole will recognize my demands in this asymmetrical relationship. According to Max Stirner's model, there can be only one perfect egoist. He therefore must be God and be regarded as such by the rest who accept the asymmetry in the face of His demands. A community of perfect egoists cannot exist without the desires of each one of them being constantly frustrated. The antics of a spoiled child may be effective for as long as it is under the care of adults; in a community of spoiled children none attains its desired goal. The cynicism and ruthlessness of adults are the characteristics of spoiled children who count on the fact that the rest of humanity will indefinitely consist of indulgent adults. As the number of spoiled children increases and there are fewer adults at hand, the children lose ground and can only explain their failures as due to their not being spoiled enough.

3

Stagnant communities were sustained by conservative mythologies that primarily created obligations which called upon every individual to be concerned with the community. They imposed responsibility for values codified in myths and guarded the existing order against the disintegrating actions of creativity, intelligence, and criticism. A community in which each individual tries to avoid responsibility for the rest, and in which the obligating myths are dying out, is more inclined to rely upon another type of myth: myths of the future which belongs to the stronger. Communities of perfect conformist-egoists are the easiest prey of mythologies which—like chauvinist fanaticisms—promise to fulfill the exclusive egoistical desires of each, thanks to the total conformity of all. An aggressive conformism differs from a conservative conformism *inter alia* because it is able to appeal to private interests which become indistinguishable from commonly shared values. The aggressive myth, capable of maintaining the community in a tension of struggle and danger, is unable to maintain it outside that tension because by abandoning the cult of tradition, it is with difficulty that it retains the bond-creating values, which are effective only because they are rooted in a mythological continuity, in an inheritance of cultic consciousness.

I have to stress this difference, which in any event is a concession to the indeterminacy and ambiguity connected with the popular usage of such terms as "myth" and "mythology." For, I repeat, I use these terms in their proper meaning with reference to situations which precede empirical reality and empirical time, but which give them a coherent meaning and create a nontemporal paradigm removed from real becoming—a paradigm which it is necessary in real becoming *to equal*. Both narratives that constitute religious mythologies, and philosophical assumptions which perceive a gradual fulfillment in cultural realities of non-historical essences (the nature of humanity, the essence of thought, the essence of law, transcendental values, and so on) fall under this heading. In these mythologies, perfection is fulfilled in Being which antedates history, while myth shows us that nontemporal model which we have to emulate. The existing empirical world is always a place of exile, and this awareness has to impose on each one of us individually a task to perform and a responsibility for nonpersonal values codified in myth. The function of mythical consciousness is primarily to awaken the sense of obligation, of a *consciousness of indebtedness* towards Being, and this consciousness may create a reciprocal bond of actual assistance among the participants in the debt, even though this bond is instinctively opposed to change. The term "myth" is also commonly used to designate a contrary consciousness: the *consciousness of a creditor*. Myths which are directed mainly towards a future utopia, which is to honor as yet unfulfilled claims; myths, which principally codify *demands* rather than *obligations*, contain their own poisons. These are different from the poisons of conservative myths, since a community of grievances, by virtue of its own contents, must appeal to the idea of a chosen people and also binds the elect in the hope of fulfilling their demands, that is, it creates a bond in whose content are values opposed to the bond, namely, private aspirations which divide the group. In such myths, elements which refer to the past, serve only as additional sanctions for the demands and not as a justification for obligations. The first category of myths chiefly provides an understanding of the existing world through a reference to an initial mythical situation, and it identifies the principles which govern this understanding with the collection of existing values, which demand to be accepted as objects of care and do not demand creativity. The second offers a perspective by organizing resentments and upholding all emotions associated with a sense of unjustified degradation.

It is true that the boundary between these two variants of mythology is not in fact drawn as clearly as one might suppose from its abstract description; and the simultaneous presence of both types of emotions in a single, mythologically self-determined community is not only possible but common. But the distinction is not without significance, if only in the form of an idealized model which allows us to trace the dominance of either one or the other variety. The Christian myth, which is the second mythopoeic attempt after the Buddhist one to cover the whole human species, rather than a single ethnically defined community, has undergone an evolution in which the dominant presence of the first model has given way to the second, although both were always active in that myth. Jesus demanded that one should first be reconciled with one's brother before proceeding with sacrifices to God. He made available an ethnic myth to the whole world made equal in the same conscious awareness of sin; he regarded every human being, and not just members of his own race, as neighbors. By in turn becoming the focus of a new myth of redemption, he initiated a community which had hammered its spiritual relationship with him into the idea of a new chosen people equipped with the right to conquer the world. Once the Church began to imitate the Roman Empire in its administrative structure and itself began to take over the imperial functions, the idea of the private saintliness of each Christian individual became fixed as a principle of education. Saintliness became that private interest which was to secure overall conformity. The myth of debtors distinguished in the world by the self-knowledge of their own sinfulness grew into a myth of saints whose apparently similar self-knowledge allowed them to legalize their claims to authority over mankind. The ideal of neighborly love gave way to the ideal of one's own saintliness achievable within a framework of a perfect conformity. Apologists will doubtless say that these ideals are not in conflict but fit together perfectly, bound with the tie of ends and means, since Christianity teaches that one's own saintliness is acquired through the love of one's neighbor. It is however a doctrinal congruity, contradicted by pedagogical realities. For, in fact, there is a profound difference between urging every individual that his ultimate goal is the acquisition of saintliness through total obedience (which among other requirements, also includes love of one's neighbor), on each occasion interpreted ad hoc by the superiors according to the demands of the moment and recommending the love and succor of one's neighbor without conditions as an end rather than as means. The neighbor, who is only a means to my own saintliness, only the compost on which my angelic properties are to blossom, cannot seriously be the object of my concern and responsibility—also when, or especially when, I have to hand manuals of saintliness which always inevitably serve to find an interpretation of the commands which is most favorable to me. An education which teaches that each individual's most important aim is to become perfect, naturally multiplies sanctimonious bigots convinced of their saintliness. I am to care for myself—and for my neighbors to the extent that they enter into a calculation of my salvation. But my neighbors too crucially need help in salvation, so there is no better way for me to demonstrate my love for them than by preaching at them. If they do not wish to listen, they are themselves to blame, and in any event any coercion will be for their own good. This is a brief, but far from distorted, sketch of Christian education in force for centuries and codified in moral theology, an education aimed at shaping the perfect egoists-conformists. Christianity will not be able to abandon it completely until it realizes how much evil has been produced by the ideal of private saintliness offered to each individual as an ultimate goal; until we also come to understand the intimate link which binds that ideal with the fact that Christianity created the first European models of the totalitarian state; that it was probably unique in human history in not only practicing but also openly declaring the principle, according to which what we see as white should be called black, if that is what the authorities demand. According to

St Ignatius's famous formula: "We have to conform to the Catholic Church in such a way that if something it has defined as black appears white to our eyes, we have to call it black."

I am again rehearsing discoveries made long ago, but I think they deserve repetition. I am not at all concerned with the history of Christianity, which I well know would receive an extraordinarily one-sided and unjust treatment if one were to target it on this educational model, ignoring the vast accumulation of effort in thought and feeling which repeatedly upset that model, while claiming its authority from the same source. What I am concerned with is a confrontation between two types of education rooted in two types of mythology. Such a confrontation is important in a situation in which the awareness by people of participation in one species and their awareness of the dependence which links the fate of all participants in that species, has become common for the first time.

4

As we have already remarked, all projective and aggressive myths appealed to the notion of a chosen people, at least when they passed from the dream stage to the practical stage. On the face of it, we should be led to believe that in the longed-for paradise of united humanity the projective myths would be well-suited to organize the human commonwealth, which as a totality would declare itself the chosen people, and would therefore as a totality continue its conquistadorial campaign against nature, and would succeed in retaining a permanent bond with a species-promethianism without a need for a conservative cult of tradition and without fear of the relativity of knowledge.

Experience, however, does not incline towards a strong belief in this perspective. A rationalized community—that is, a commonwealth in which nonproductive and nonlegal bonds have withered and in which the will to cooperate is also strong enough to assure constructive collective work on the basis of a purely rational calculation and to diffuse conflicts—such a commonwealth seems to be possible only to the extent that the Enlightenment metaphysic of basic harmony of individual and collective interests in all spheres of life is true. Anyone capable of taking this metaphysic seriously—who therefore believes that human interests, when properly understood, are not really in conflict and that disagreements arise out of errors of calculation or out of subscription to chimerical and opposed doctrines which people choose to inflict upon each other—is also entitled to believe that a world cleared of philosophical illusions, myths, the weight of tradition, the cult of irrational tribal, national, religious, and family ties, will result in a conflict-free cooperation based on a proper coordination of egoisms. In societies organized rationally from a legal point of view, educational institutions would, according to this doctrine, be concerned to demonstrate to everyone the fundamental coherence of egoisms and explain that an egoism, targeted at other people, inevitably turns against itself; that therefore my interest is secured most profitably when I do not impair others' interests. If such a doctrine, which constitutes the proper substance of utilitarian programs, is correct, we can therefore count on an enlightened humanity which will secure itself a harmony just on the basis of legal bonds and a rational calculus of profits and losses, without having to refer to specifically ethical motivations, to values not linked to self-interest, or to mythical justifications of these values (and there are no justifications outside the mythical).

This optimistic philosophy has admittedly received too many wounds, both theoretical and experiential, for us to be able to discover in contemporary literature an account of it as full of lofty *naiveté* as we know from the writings of Helvetius and Bentham. It nevertheless continues to offer a permanent background to all visions of the future world from which a scientific organization of life will simultaneously remove mythologies, deprivation, and social conflicts; and where the level of social enlightenment alone will effectively defend the public good against the excesses of antisocial individuals, since antisocial behavior will automatically rebound on the perpetrator.

Although created by spokesmen for enlightened liberalism and lovers of public liberties, the philosophy of fundamental harmony covering all individual interests is in fact the most perfect rationalization of a totalitarian state that one can imagine. Moreover, it is such, although for different reasons, in both its variants—as a social program and as a metaphysical assumption. Both these variants, both interpretations of the principle of fundamental harmony, merit a brief description.

The first interpretation has the following sense: if my behavior, directed against the interests of other people, brings me benefits, this happens because of defects in the social institutions. Rationally ordered social institutions are sufficient to remove the conflicts of warring egoisms by bringing it about that no one gains by acting against others. In this simple-mindedly sketched form the theory of fundamental harmony becomes the basis for a program of a rational and conflictless society. But the moralists, philosophers, and utopian socialist reformers, who placed their hopes in just such a social transformation, when they pondered the ways of bypassing interpersonal clashes, had in mind various circumstances: most frequently conflicts connected with the presence of private property or conflicts manifesting themselves in lawbreaking and crime. They were not always able to perceive clearly the following circumstance: the social institutions, which might have breathed life into the ideals of fundamental harmony, would have had to remove the possibility of all competition between human beings and would therefore be assuming a community so undifferentiated that no member of it could possibly seek anything that might possibly distinguish him from the rest. In other words, it would therefore be a society without any values which distinguished an individual in relation to the rest, since each distinguishing value—in the sphere of prestige, power, possession and skills—is inevitably the focus of competition and creates conflict-tensions in at least this sense—that in seeking it I seek to exclude others from its benefits. A society which succeeded in bringing about this state would have had to abandon all values which could not be shared by all, and would therefore need to arrive at a state of total uniformity among individuals—as envisaged in the models of Enlightenment utopians. Dom Deschamps's terrifying ideal of perfect totalitarianism—a society consisting of clones identically attired, identical in life style, modes of thought, feelings, desires, and even physical appearance—is in fact an attempt at a rational application of assumptions round which noble liberals wove their political thoughts; perhaps the only attempt where the creator did not flinch from completing his ideal, whereby the sources of conflicts and competition among men would be finally eliminated.

Someone might respond that, while this ideal may seem nightmarish to us, we cannot exclude in advance the possibility of a shift, as a result of which it would not only be brought to life, but would actually guarantee people complete satisfaction, if their education could so organize their needs that they would experience no distress in this total identification of each with all, and would lead their lives in a blissful sense of plenitude.

Such reflections may appear an empty fantasy, but this is only because of the colossal distance between this ideal and our world of values. But this distance is probably no greater than the one which separates the existential horizons of tenth-century Europeans, traditionally the *saeculum obscurum,* from the horizons of thinking elites of our own civilization. Let us therefore take seriously for a moment the utopia of a conflictless society, from which the possibility of competitive situations has been removed because the values distinguishing individuals have been eliminated from people's minds, and let us assume that it can be brought to life.

We can observe at once that the community we have thus established in imagination would live in a universal and perfect stagnation because it would not feel, either as a whole or in any of its elements, any need for change. Its technology would necessarily be purely reproductive. A culture transcending the instrumental functions connected with the needs of organic life would die out, since dissatisfaction is the sole source of cultural creativity in all its realms. One can of course declare that cultural fertility and technological progress are not values in themselves, and are therefore not values at all in a society in which the needs which set a price on them had disappeared, for progress can only appear as a value by reference to unsatisfied needs. But what compels our belief that the multiplication of needs, rather than their restriction, is itself worthy of support?

However, this hypothetical argument turns against itself. A society in which all sources of change had dried up—where therefore satisfaction is general and complete—would, irrespective of the level of needs at which this satisfaction came about, be defenseless in the face of every new situation which (for whatever reason) were to disturb its stagnant duration. It would, for instance, be unable to respond to any threat from the natural environment. For that reason it is unimaginable, or rather imaginable only in conditions under which the natural environment were to acquiesce in a similar immobility. Each situation calling upon inventiveness which mobilized the creative, and not just the reproductive, potentialities of the community would amount to an annihilation of the life principle of that community, assuming it was prepared to cope with this reversal (or the annihilation of the community itself, were it ready to perish rather than change). The supposition that stagnant societies have endured for millennia has no argumentative force, because we conventionally call "stagnant" societies which experience a slow level of change, and we do not know of any societies that are stagnant in the precise sense of the word. Furthermore, humanity, all of whose elements are mutually dependent and also incapable of life without the already accumulated technological resources, is no longer capable of recreating its pristine natural environment—being unlike a primitive nomad group which is able to exploit progressively, apparently without end, the still unpopulated natural areas which differ little from one another.

In other words: the ideally conflictless society assumes a situation in which individuals have been deprived of all possibility of choice and therefore also of creativity. The creative possibility is thereby removed from society as a whole.

However we were to imagine the instruments that would sustain this state of perfect stagnation—be it in the form of repressive measures or in an internalized readiness to identify the individual completely with the totality—it would be a state which we would be fully entitled to call the end of the human world.

5

And now, here is the second metaphysical version of the principle of fundamental harmony under discussion. It is found in Rousseau and, derivatively in this respect, in Fichte. Briefly, it assumes that humanity is an irremovable nature of each individual, that therefore in each individual one may discover, as a proper and constitutive attribute, a boundless solidarity with the species. Conflicts are symptomatic of social pathology, the outcome of a failure or depravity in social institutions which dehumanizes individuals, blunting their proper calling to a harmonious willing cooperation.

The dangers contained in this optimistic faith in man's innate natural goodness are as great as those produced by a seemingly opposite doctrine. In fact, whether we say that people are naturally selfish and we decide to construct a program of general harmony which would accommodate the conflicting egoisms; or whether, on the contrary, we declare that human nature is altruistic and decide to build our hopes of the perfect society upon it—the outcome of both these barren and empty principles would be the same. In saying that the disinterested readiness to identify with humanity constitutes each individual's nature, we imply that all the means with which we would guide people towards a conflictless life would simply be a revelation of that hidden nature that is "in me". Action which reveals their authentic nature, their primordial calling, cannot be inimical to human beings; what makes a human being human cannot be evil. Therefore every form of coercion, forcing behavior towards the general good, has to be supported. ("One must compel to freedom," according to Jean Jacques's famous formula.) Humanity resides in everyone, but not everyone is aware of it. The enlightened therefore have a right to humanize the unenlightened—using force if other methods fail. This is indeed a peculiar interpretation of that metaphysic of "humanity in man," an interpretation which admittedly is not inevitable, but is nevertheless possible and, as we know, is in fact exemplified in history. In any event, the idea which turns man into a "natural altruist" is not in any way secure in its content from a totalitarian interpretation—just like the apparently opposing picture of "egoistic nature," which has either to be tamed or to be integrated into a conflictless order.

In fact, conflicts are the product of differentiation, without which neither culture nor technological development can exist. This trivial observation does not imply any doctrine concerning "innate selfishness" or man's inevitable (since biologically determined) aggressiveness, or the intrinsically adversarial character of human encounters. It does not imply either Hobbes's or Freud's or Sartre's anthropology. It only assumes that the removal of conflict from communal life is a deceptive hope which would be in the highest degree dangerous if it were submitted to a practical test.

Conflicts and competition are therefore inevitable in every civilization capable of life. That is precisely why it is frivolous to hope that communal life may function efficiently within an organization based on a model of self-regulating structures, with a complete absence of those nonreplicating and nonutilitarian solidarity bonds which bear fruit only on a mythical tree.

6

At the same time, all those who warn against the threat of myth will be right. Myth can be threatening in many ways—for example, by its tendency to limitless expansion. A myth may grow like a tumor: it may seek to replace positivistic knowledge and laws, may attempt forcibly to take over almost all areas of culture, and may become encrusted in despotism, terror, and mendacity. It also threatens to relieve its participants of responsibility for their own situation, drain away the desire for freedom, and bring the value of freedom as such under suspicion.

The valid need for myth, set against a valid self-defense against the threat of myth is a collision which constitutes the sensitive area of our civilization, its poisoned tissue, and its embarrassing illness. As I said, to the extent that it is successful, the flight from myth becomes a surrender in the face of the pressure of immediate facts, an assent to a perpetual distraction, an acceptance of a life which glides along in a succession of events, each of which is self-exhausting and which in total do not refer to anything. It is the terror in the face of the inquiry regarding the contingency of the world and seeks ways of dampening that terror; it cannot be free of deception. Most often the search for myth is an attempt to discover a caring authority which easily deals with ultimate questions, equips with stable hierarchies of value, surrounds one with a thicket of signposts, relieves one of liberty, wraps one up again in a cocoon of infancy, and satisfies a lazy need for submission; but a satisfaction which is acquired in this manner is also not free of deception.

Is it possible for a myth to operate in its socially indispensable function without the threat of mythological terror? And, analogously, can there be an attitude which consents to a participation in a mythically defined human fellowship without using this participation as an excuse for avoiding responsibility for one's life? In other words, is it possible simultaneously to avoid a life anaesthetized by daily events, insensitive to the attraction of the mythical abyss, and at the same time to avoid a life numbed by the deadly certainty of myth slumbering in its benign barrenness?

In attempting to answer this question two circumstances are important. First, it is almost impossible to program a myth effectively while assuming its purely instrumental value; it is impossible to decree it. Second, the content of myths cannot include guarantees against interpretations which would turn them into organs of repression and despotism—even though we have to admit that the content of many known myths are more or less susceptible to such interpretations.

If then, among the social functions of myths, there are those which are irreplaceable and specific—apart from the instrumental functions which myths perform in relation to all branches of life—the very presence of these functions cannot determine the limits of a malignant growth of mythology. What we know for certain is that in maintaining any kind of human fellowship we need a faith in ready-made and nonarbitrary values, and that at the same time it is dangerous to believe that these values are at any time fixed and completed, that they can relieve one of situational interpretations and a situational responsibility for them. A mythology can be socially fruitful only when it is unceasingly suspect, constantly subject to vigilance which would frustrate its natural tendency to turn into a narcotic. We know that it is possible for an individual to maintain this vigilance. We do not know for certain whether this is possible in the operation of a myth within a social rhythm; or at least whether it is possible other than through a division of labor which assigns to some the one-sided dignity of the guardians of myth, while to the others the one-sided dignity of its critics.

Myths are a source of a dangerous intoxication whenever they serve as defense against anxiety and in that function they demand counteraction. A total taming of the world and a total elimination of its otherness may be only an illusion and is not always free of bad faith. Mythological interpretations of the world are capable of helping to remove this otherness to the extent that this is possible, and they are also capable of helping us to understand why this is not possible in full. Myths which perform these two irremovable and irreplaceable functions cannot create a sense of satiety. They always contain within themselves a version of the Myth of the Cave, some variant of the story of paradise lost, a sense of the inability of a harmonious transition from a conditioned to an unconditioned Being. They reiterate the bitter *Lama sabachtani?* ("Why hast Thou forsaken me?") and the promise of an escape from the Cave is unclear and uncertain.

7

We do not of course know the mythological future of our civilization. I have in mind mythologies in the narrower sense, that is, religious mythologies. Presently, there are alive on earth two mythological organisms which have succeeded in transcending the local restrictions of their genealogy and in universalizing their myths to a scale of unrestricted openness: Christianity and Buddhism. Although split internally and full of degenerate growths at their peripheries, both therefore satisfy an indispensable, although far from sufficient, condition for the vigor in a civilization in which the basic resources of spiritual life are slowly losing their folkloristic color. Both have demonstrated a certain ability to penetrate the world of civilizations alien to those in which they were conceived. Furthermore, Buddhism (which, as mythology and not just as an object of study, had at first permeated Europe in a curiously deformed theosophical variant) has for some time now been the center of modest attraction in its Zen version. This last is probably easier to accept within an industrial civilization because it can be cultivated in the fever of daily tasks, and does not demand a monklike contemplative segregation.

The undoubted decline of religious life in recent years, almost automatically associated with the advance of urbanization and general education, does not deserve to be turned into a linear law of history. History is full of examples of undoubted degeneracy in particular areas of culture—in the plastic arts, scientific thought, religion, and law—and usually they can be interpreted as crises of maladjustment. Witnesses sensitive to old values might have seen these crises as symptoms of the final withering of these forms of culture, but succeeding generations knew them only as inescapable phases of a decline preceding new forms.

The waning of the Scholastic model of Christianity appears irreversible. I have in mind the model which attempted to turn mythology into a fully accredited element of knowledge, and at the same time to turn institutionalized myth into an administrator of earthly life. But the violent speed of retreat from such an interpretation in the Catholic religion in recent years testifies to Catholicism's amazing plasticity. Propositions which a few years ago sounded like sinister heresies have become a currency allowed at least to circulate, even if not universally accepted. All prophesies regarding the future fate of this situation would be willful. But it is unlikely that some as yet nonexistent mythology, that is, one which would not appeal to an existing mythological treasury but would proclaim a revelation freshly divulged by a divinity, could conquer significant areas of contemporary culture. Mahomet was the last prophet in history who had succeeded in this—the last who had not confined himself to an interpretation of an already existing myth but had proclaimed himself the messenger of a new revelation, and who also succeeded in imposing his mythology on large areas of the world. Numberless crowds of later prophets, who assured people that they were drawing new inspiration from supernatural sources, disappeared without a trace or at best produced tiny sects which soon dried up in the world's indifference. All significant religious revolutions and schisms occurring in the last thirteen centuries were not, in their mythological claims, attempts at finding new sources of God's word. On the contrary, they appealed to existing myth, in which they merely tried to reinstate its original meaning and a proper dignity unsullied by human spite. In any event, this appears to be a natural property in the life of religious myth: if it is to retain its reality in the souls of the faithful, the moment of original revelation should rather disappear in the undefined darkness of past ages, dissolve in some misty "once upon a time" at the source of history. Only exceptionally do we see acts of new revelation which were both historically fixed and successful. But they too were—as in the case of Jesus and Mahomet—the superstructure and the reinterpretation of an earlier revelation.

It is only upon this, an admittedly flimsy basis, of a centuries-long absence of new and successful revelations, that we are entitled to speculate that future metamorphoses of mythology would be reforms, that is, attempts at a return to old sources, attempts at reinterpretation of the existing heritage, and would be extensions of existing beliefs.

We cannot now imagine a return to myths which could effectively reinstate a hierocratic despotism over secular life. But neither can we imagine a culture totally bereft of mythological elements. The principles of coexistence between mythology and a scientifically controlled civilization will undoubtedly be worked out over a long period marked by tensions and clashes. But the appearance of such principles does not seem impossible, though it is unlikely that they would contain a guarantee of perpetual harmony. That is because a myth, which is to locate empirical facts in an unconditioned order, inevitably contains the act of questioning the palpable world, because it always presents that world as non-self-sufficient and devoid of its own value, endowed with values thanks only to its tie with nontemporal realities.

But this act of questioning conditioned Being may be variously articulated. It may be a principle of an eternal hatred of incurably sick flesh; it may therefore cause people to flee the world, to seek asylum in closed enclaves of perfection. This principle gave rise to ascetic sects and contemplative orders absorbed in self-admiration, insensitive to temporal matters and even loath to proselytize.

One can also question the empirical world in projects which wish to submit earthly realities to the tyranny of saintliness and impose upon the visible embodiments of the invisible world a legislative and executive power with respect to human societies. Despotic variants of religious universalism in great mythologies arose on this principle. It is hard to believe that questioning the empirical world in these terms could have a chance of success in the currently flourishing civilization.

If, however, mythologies do not wish either to advocate flight from the world or theocracy, there are still other ways in which they can question all the realities of immediate experience: by demonstrating the non-self-sufficiency of such realities—their inability to create independently those values thanks to which human communities are able to survive, their failure at self-interpretation, and their failure to produce by their own strength principles of understanding the world in addition to rules for manipulating objects.

Mythologies which would wish to be just this: principles for understanding things in their preempirical order; reserves of fundamental values which do not prejudice every single situation but demand that they be situationally interpreted; instruments of relativization of empirical occurrences. Such mythologies can coexist with a civilization which is scientifically regulated and tireless in the multiplication of technological resources. They need not paralyze its growth. Should any of the existing mythological organisms be seized with an unbending will favoring such principles of coexistence with civilization, we may assume that such an organism may survive.

10

THE PERMANENCE AND FRAGILITY OF MYTH

1

We have already discussed the various motives active in the production of myths and in maintaining their vitality. One might, however, suppose that these are transient motives, that is, ones that are tied to modes of thought, ways of asking questions, to sentiments or conceptual nets which are created anew in historically relative civilizational formations. At the foundations of the mythical organization of the world one could therefore perhaps discern either artificial needs, which intellectual progress would eliminate, or transient instruments of social life, civilizationally defined, useful only under certain conditions, expendable at other times.

Hence it might be instructive to reflect on the question whether it is possible to point to such a quality permanently connected with humanity, which might be regarded as a fixed store of mythopoeic energy. I tried to point to the phenomenon of the world's indifference which might be regarded as the most fundamental circumstance from this point of view. But this phenomenon itself, to be intelligible, refers to some specifically and irremovably human qualities.

Someone might say—and many indeed have said it—that the needs and behavior which appear to be specifically human are always capable of interpretation as continuations, particularizations, differentiations, and refinements of animal needs. The seventeenth-century dispute over the boundary between animal and human intelligence is continuing, and although it now relies on a different and incomparably richer argumentation, it seems in its ultimate conclusions to reveal philosophical preferences. Human competences may be animalized totally, that is, one could find biologically functional equivalents for all competences, even when one acknowledges (as Julian Huxley does) the emergence of man as a turning point in evolution.

Human communal life ordered according to well-defined principles is not a specifically human invention. Fear of death is, we may surmise, common in nature; common at least is the behavior which we are entitled to interpret as manifestation of fear. Sexually oriented behavior (that is, a biologically designated area of human life) may, it seems, suffice to illuminate all subtleties of the love experience and its expression within our species. The production of science may also be explained (following Mach's assumptions) as an extension of biological defense tools for which the human species had merely discovered efficient, previously unknown, modes of social accumulation and transmission in the form of speech, writing, and economizing inductive generalizations. From this point of view, the ability to generate scientific theories is a shorthand technique of recording the performed experiments. In a theoretical production the human community makes use of the same competence which is available to all organisms endowed with a nervous system, that is, makes use of an ability to acquire conditioned reflexes. Just as a nervous system spontaneously decides that, given a certain number of connections between phenomena, it pays to record them in the form of a trace, to regard them as provisionally permanent (with of course the possibility of a recall, that is, the extinction of the reflex), society—through science, its thought tool—evaluates the observed regularities in nature, and in the same manner produces criteria which establish the threshold of the rentability of the theories. It therefore fixes the conditions in which these regularities ought provisionally to be accepted as immutable. Such criteria are nothing but rules for accepting or rejecting judgments, that is, a logic of probabilistic reasoning. The additional meaning which is ascribed to them as criteria of truth and falsity is a metaphysical fantasy, if the concept of truth signifies anything other than "a judgment which it is worth accepting on account of accumulated experience."

Also, such apparently exclusively human qualities like moral scruples in social relations have their far-reaching analogies in the behavior of animals. The German ethologist, Konrad Lorenz, has indicated in *The Expression of the Emotions in Man and Animals* that all species—the predators in particular—are equipped with inhibiting mechanisms which distinctly make it difficult to kill and maim members of one's own species (although in the case of domesticated animals there is often a psychopathic weakening or disappearance of these inhibitors). There is even the connected phenomenon in animals of the "submissive posture," visible when, for example, a dog which is being attacked stops motionless and exposes its jugular vein, that part of its body which demands the greatest protection, thus releasing an inhibiting mechanism in the aggressor. According to Lorenz, man's various conventional, ethical, and intellectual properties display a striking similarity to the properties which appear in domesticated animals, in contrast to wild animals. These include the loss of selectivity in reacting to stimuli which provoke definite endogenous reactions only in specific combinations. The domestication of animals is associated with a hypertrophy of those arousal processes which belong to the oldest phylogenetic layers connected with feeding and breeding, and with the weakening of newer, more differentiated forms of behavior such as family ties and social behavior reactions in general. The evolution of man as a domesticated animal appears to follow the same direction. Moral, as well as aesthetic, sensibility appears to be the self-defense of the species against degenerative effects of domestication: the morally valued modes of behavior are precisely those which are threatened by the domestication process, that is, readiness for sacrifice, determination in the defense of the family, and so on. The morally suspect tendencies are those whose growth one observes in domestic animals. Similarly, aesthetic valuation, at least the common one, prefers those physical properties of men and animals which resist domestication. Paradoxically, for instance, we regard as "beastly" excessive sexual readiness, which in fact constitutes the specific characteristic of domesticated animals and of man as one of them. In other words, culture replaces instincts which are necessary for the preservation of the species and which are weakened in the domestication process.

Also (according to the same author) that most human of human characteristics, disinterested curiosity—an active interest in a biologically indifferent environment, an interest thanks to which culture could come about and the notion of creativity thus acquire a meaning in relation to human behavior—even this characteristic, which appears to us a radical departure from the animal kingdom, is capable of interpretation in zoological categories. The absence of a rigorous life specialization, of exactly demarcated adaptation to defined conditions, and therefore a versatility, an adaptive plasticity, and an ability to organize life under the most varied conditions is shared by our species with (for instance) the brown rat. The exploration of unknown elements of the environment—not because they are threatening or because they hold out a promise of satisfying immediate hungers—has a clear biological sense, but is possible only in creatures whose organs are constructed in a nonspecialized way and are suitable for the most diverse applications. Such a "theoretical" posture enables some animals, as well as man, to discover in the environment properties capable of practical exploitation which were not previously known and were not correlated with any innate mechanisms of adaptation. Common among young mammals is an active, disinterested curiosity directed at the world, which normally disappears when they attain maturity and which therefore constitutes an evolutionary phase that gives way to systematic reactions of fear in the face of new and unknown stimuli. A distinctive feature of humans (and of certain other species) is the so-called neotenia, that is, the preservation of these youthful characteristics in maturity and old age, as if in this respect humans were arrested at a teenage phase. Also in the shape of the skull, the type of hair covering, pigmentation, the relative weight of the brain, the structure of the female sexual organs the human species displays a characteristic fixation at the immature or even embryonic stage (the "fetalization" of the species) which in an overwhelming number of mammals disappears with age. Thus, a childlike physical build coincides with childlike behavioral characteristics; man's eternal immaturity, his permanent incompletion, constitutes the fundamental condition of creativity and many-sidedness, an ability to test the world and a curiosity about the world; the physical and behavioral characteristics of neotenia, absent in creatures living in the wild, are perceptible, to varying degrees, in tamed species of animals. In human creativity and freedom one can detect an extension of play behavior which generally disappears in mammals once they cross the threshold of maturity, to be replaced by a rigidified system of responses.

But all these manifestations of permanent infantilism—freedom, plasticity, incompleteness, many-sidedness—are not only a constitutive source of human culture and expansion. Just because they prevent the achievement of a permanent biological balance, they are also a reservoir of enormous risk. They have destroyed the animal paradise which maintains a constant identity between inclinations and obligations, they have blocked various beneficial, instinctual automatisms and have damaged the motor regulations of relationships within the species. The aggressive stand has lost its old biological sense, whereby it was directed against threats from other species, and has seemingly transferred its energy (now, from a biological point of view, in a quite senseless form) onto ties between groupings within the species. The endogenous breaks preventing the destruction of members of one's own species are not only weakened in the natural process of domestication; they are also absent in the case of behavior which employs artificially constructed destructive and defensive tools, since these are not, so to say, envisaged in the construction of the organisms. Hence the constant conflict between moral restraints, which replace nonexistent or impoverished innate reserves serving to defend the species, and the transposed aggressive responses. Together with freedom, domestication brought man pathological hereditary changes and lethal factors requiring constant counteraction.

I have summarized this thesis of an eminent ethologist because it seems to me important in relation to two fundamental questions directed, from two opposite intellectual directions, at the mythical organization of the world. Can we interpret the social secretions of mythical products by reference to a permanent human situation in nature? Do we need myth to interpret our natural situation? These two questions give birth to a third: Can we without contradiction (or without a vicious circle) comprehend myth in its biological functions and also comprehend our own biology mythically?

Even if that situation of permanent incompletion which, according to Pico della Mirandola, endows humanity with dignity can be biologically described, if our freedom and our creativity are rooted in the biological peculiarities of the species, and if the price for these gains is the loss of a spontaneous ability to regulate our relationships within our species, then indeed cultural norms become the indispensable substitute for innate rules and mechanisms which defend the species from self-destruction. If in turn (as we already said) the social inheritance of these norms may be effective only within the framework of mythical constructs, then mythology would appear to be a permanent element of culture. Culture need not be regarded—as Freud would have it—only as a tool repressing instinct. It is also a tool which replaces instinctual abilities.

2

Perhaps, however, the account of this clash between nature and culture permits a certain interpretation which takes us further than the discipline of the ethologist allows. Together with tools which make possible an active, physical transformation of the natural environment, we humans have also acquired the tools of spiritual distance in relation to that environment and in relation to ourselves as part of it. It is not the fact that we are feeling and sensitive *subjects* that distinguishes us among living creatures, but the fact that we can be *objects* for ourselves, that is, be capable of splitting our consciousness so that it becomes its own observer; so that we not only have an understanding attitude towards the world but so that we have an understanding attitude towards that understanding; that we not only know that we are in the world but that we are the ones who know that we know, or rather, that we are conscious of being a consciousness. Having made our own relation to nature indirect thanks to the production of tools, we have also made our attitude to ourselves mediated. Thereby our presence in nature has ceased to be an obvious given of nature itself, not requiring explanation. Contact with nature is not per se comprehensible, because even though we understand that contact we are unable to identify permanently our own observing consciousness with our own consciousness as an element of nature under observation. Our life in culture is incapable of being nonreflectingly accepted as a continuation of a natural ecological situation, as it contains the unceasing memory of the observer doubling himself in a projection towards himself as an object. Even if we did know precisely who we are in nature, we would be unable to cease knowing that we do know—and this state of duality is enough to prevent our being completely integrated into the order of nature with which we identify in reflection but not in reflecting upon reflection.

In a word: because human beings have become objects for their own consciousness, they have become incomprehensible to themselves as subjects. In this bifurcation the subjectivity has ceased to be a part of nature, and biological determinations, to the extent that they are components of self-awareness, have ceased to be natural; they demand an interpretation. The technological conquest of the environment, together with the experimental and theoretical work which makes it possible, may be included in the evolution of animal competences and may be efficient without epistemological justifications. However, the theoretical consciousness as such, turned upon itself, cannot understand that turning back upon itself as an instance of technological activity. Demanding from itself an understanding of itself, consciousness also demands that understanding be possible in relation to acts in which it comes to know nature. It therefore produces a mythological value of truth and endows with this value the results of its own labors. Similarly, a loving human relationship may as an object be understood as an instance of a phenomenon known universally in nature. However, the circumstance that love is not only experienced but that the very fact of its experiencing is also experienced as an object, demands an interpretation which reaches towards mythological symbols, since this circumstance is beyond nature. Similarly, death is a common phenomenon of life and in this form there is nothing mysterious in human death. For an observing consciousness the disappearance of an observed consciousness is contained in the natural order; but its own anticipated death appears as violence against the nature of things, since that consciousness itself, in its distance from its own objective existence transcends that natural order.

The awareness of one's own being in the world itself therefore transcends the being in the world, and is an irreversible abandonment of the spontaneous consent to its natural position; it is the irreversible loss of a ready-made location in nature. By the very fact that it arises, the consciousness of being in the world makes consciousness inexplicable by reference to the world. Humanity ceases to be explicable for itself and must either shoulder its absoluteness, that is, accept that it explains nature in relation to itself and not the other way round, or seek self-placement through a relation to the prenatural and prehistorical reality of myth. One can reserve the privilege of the absolute—towards which a temptation of a radical historical monism leads—only at the price of radical skepticism; but radical skepticism, if it faces up to the consequences, means the ruin of the values which sustain the nonrational bonds within the human species; it therefore means the suicide of the species.

The situation I have described, which philosophers have known for a long time, may clarify the spiritual path which the mythological endeavor traverses, namely, the road upon which the constitutive stage is the phenomenon of the world's indifference. A place can be found for mythology which is not only designated by the needs of species survival, but is also a source lodged in the need for self-designation by denaturalized consciousness. The doubling of consciousness in the self-objectifying movement—an inescapable correlate of culture—creates, as already indicated, a radical self-knowledge of one's own otherness in relation to nature, of one's own nonparticipation in its order. This duality presents the world as precisely that which I am not, as a phenomenon which is primarily characterized by its inability to absorb my existence; it is therefore characterized as otherness, indifference, and passivity. The whole philosophical tradition for which inertia and passivity—purely negative descriptions—constituted physical reality, was an attempt at describing this situation; at finding words which define existence as a reality not reducible to individuation within the species. Such attempts are the obverse of the same effort which seeks to name humanity's nonrootedness in nonhuman Being.

However, to be rooted in Being which transcends me seems to be an irremovable need. The abandonment of a prereflective integration in nature cannot be taken as an irreversible situation, since it amounts to my consent to being an absolute. I cannot give this consent in good faith, that is, I cannot in good faith acknowledge that I am God. I cannot accept myself as omnipotent in the order of values knowing for certain that I am not omnipotent in the order of Being. Incapable of reinstating a spontaneous immediacy in our contacts with nature, we are constrained to seek integration in the opposite direction. Having lost the roots of our own consciousness in nature, we try to find roots for nature which would make it possible to make it like consciousness, that is, to include it in a mythical order. Reintegration, which is unattainable through a retreat from humanity, is possible only thanks to the conviction that I live in a universe which can be understood as similar to me in a certain respect, primarily as equipped with essential characteristics of my continuing existence—namely, memory and anticipatory leaps into the future. Mythology as an attempt to overcome the amnesia of Being, as vanquishing the pure facticity of the world, relieves me of a situation in which I must acknowledge myself as an accidental divinity—and this paradoxical situation I am unable to take seriously.

To summarize: the sheer presence of a specifically human consciousness in the world produces an irremovable mythopoeic energy in culture, while both the bond-creating role of myth in communal life and its integrational functions in organizing personal consciousness, appear irreplaceable, and in particular irreplaceable in favor of beliefs regulated by the criteria of scientific knowledge.

3

It is here that there appears the antinomy of practical consciousness we have already referred to a number of times. Myth makes accessible to us a world in which our existence, our thoughts, and our desires, together with that world, are already referred to a nonconditioned order and thereby they can be not only known but also understood. At the same time reflection on the difficulties which arise from an existence devoid of myths enables us to trace the genesis of myth, and to place it in the functional order of our natural behavior. It reveals a wound which mythical consciousness has a power to heal. Is a consciousness possible which acknowledges this genealogy of myth and at the same time is capable of participating in myth?

On the face of it, we are not confronted here with an antinomy in the logical sense: the inquiry regarding the genesis and function of myth is logically independent from an inquiry regarding its function in understanding the world and does not prejudge any answers to it. Apparently one can, without falling into a contradiction, acknowledge the subconscious reasons which awaken the mythical imagination on the social level, and participate seriously in the products of this imagination.

In reality it is not quite like this. True, the antinomy we are discussing is not a logical antinomy, that is, it is not a cognitive situation forcing us to accept contradictory judgments. It is, however, a practical antinomy, that is, a situation which demands modes of behavior which are incompatible on psychological grounds. A real participation in myth assumes its approval in the so-called cognitive order, that is, assumes a kind of intellectual trust. A belief in a total genetic explicability of myth paralyzes that trust. Beyond verbal assurances, I am unable to reduce any contents, to which I ascribe cognitive value, to their functions *for me*. I am unable to retain the conviction if I can draw its content from noncognitive motives which force me to this conviction (whatever these motivations might be). Putting it crudely, I am, for instance, unable to hold a deep belief in divine care over the world, and at the same time to be deeply convinced that my faith is the outcome either of my life's frustrations, or of a need for care, or of membership of a community lacking in the possibility of social emancipation, or of participation in social pathologies of language, and so on.

Even so, this conflict does not appear to be the ultimate situation and this is due to reasons we have already partly discussed. These reasons are connected with the already noted mythical character of the value of truth itself. If the ultimate criteria which distinguish truth from falsity in popular and scientific thought cannot be validated without a valuing option (relevant especially to the technological applicability of knowledge), then the options which are active in the mythical order of life cannot be discriminated as worse by reference to the higher-order dominant values which would allow adjudication on both these areas. What is more, one cannot assert that the two options are mutually exclusive if neither of them aspires to exclusivity over the whole extent of spiritual life. A genetic interpretation of myth acts destructively on mythical consciousness in just the same way as the genetic interpretation of logic upon the transcendental meaning ascribed to scientific knowledge. It is true that that transcendental meaning is not a condition of effective scientific production; scientific consciousness can apparently prosper under conditions of instrumental and functional autointerpretation, which myth cannot abide. However, it is precisely in the light of this distinction that it is clear that the genetic interpretation of myth belongs to a different order of spiritual life than participation in myth; it belongs to an area subject essentially to the same criteria as the totality of discursive thought. A real—that is, by no means only a suppositional—participation in the mythical order is not in general a part of knowledge and becomes such only in degenerate variants of mythical consciousness. In its verbal realizations myth is an expression of collective experience, and participants in this experience have no obligation to place it in the same order of life in which scientific values function, or to subject them to rigors of the same criteria of affirming and denying judgments. That is why, just as it cannot lay claims to a persuasive power, myth is also insensitive (or is capable of being insensitive) to destructive reasons taken over from scientifically relevant experience. Explained genetically, it loses its vitality to the extent that mythical consciousness has already succumbed to confusion with technological consciousness—a confusion which is admittedly common but neither inescapable nor permanent, but bound to a certain specific cultural formation where technological consciousness displays a particularly intransigent rapacity, and a cult of the sciences dominates spiritual life. If, for example, religious beliefs are eroded under the influence of religious studies, the cause lies not in the nature of things or in an essential psychological divergence of both these areas, nor in their logical incompatibility, but in civilizationally defined, suicidal claims of myth to nonmythical legitimacy. Just as mythical consciousness may impose its own rules of understanding on a rationally organized world without questioning that rational organizing form, it can also acknowledge itself as a fact, as a component of a world accessible to scientific exploration, while maintaining a genetic self-understanding within its own order, that is, understanding its own presence by reference to that area of Being which saturates its own content. Thus, while the clash of myth with knowledge about myths is real, it is in each instance civilizationally defined: it is a clash within certain cultures, rather than within the universal nature of human experience.

Nevertheless, this clash is not accidental in the sense that that level of human life which sets in motion scientific and technological creativity easily collides with the mythopoeic level in every nonstagnant culture. In an active culture mythical consciousness will always be suspected of being a wasteful consumption of spiritual energy which might have been used up productively, or that it is the source of poisonous fumes in which the vitality of the human brain and muscles withers. On the other hand, since mythical consciousness is intent on exploring those areas of Being which need to be, in its view, constitutive of self-understanding, it has the innate tendency to extract the greatest possible portion of human spiritual reserves. Thus, although we may imagine a situation in which a conflict between those two layers subsides, or disappears, we cannot imagine the existence of instruments guaranteeing either a permanent and infinite harmony between them or even an eternal truce. Within a culture capable of arousing creative inventiveness, each version of harmony will be fragile, uncertain, and demanding vigilance. For this reason—rather than for the one given earlier, that is, not on account of the antinomy of mythical consciousness—the mutual suspicion of these two layers of culture may be regarded as not only an unavoidable state but as one that is positively salutary. The mythical consciousness will always emanate suspicion towards human participation in the world of nature; in our very bodiliness and its expansion it will always be seeking symptoms revealing a life of exiles, a life in decline. Mythical consciousness cannot be deprived of its aspect turned against the body, or at least against the exclusivity which the imperatives of life—that is, temporal and doomed to extinction—demand. Within the uncertainties of our efforts and desires confronted with that plenitude of satiety with which the root of Being guessed at in myth is nourished, the mythical consciousness will always be watching the ephemeral shadows flickering on the wall of the Cave.

That is why the coexistence of myth with our bodily life cannot be free of conflict. That is why a simultaneous participation in both orders will inevitably give birth to a feeling of their noncontiguity, which can be overcome only through the self-renunciation of one of the sides and this—which just now was the main object of these reflections—cannot be carried through finally, consistently, safely, and in good faith. The ideal of a perfect harmony is chimerical and, moreover, threatening because it gives birth to temptations of intolerance.

We are crowded in a world in which the all-embracing importunities of daily life tear away our moments of attentiveness upon the ultimate copingstones of life. It is easy to die before securing a breathing space for disinterested reflection. But we do not know whether it is better thus.

4

A summary explaining the questions and answers contained in all these reflections may not be out of place. I am primarily concerned to make clear that these reflections do not question—nor are they meant to confirm—any existing interpretations which refer to the social and psychological functions of religious myths. The thought developed by the Durkheim school that myths constitute media through which a community exerts an integrational pressure on its members; reflection on the therapeutic function of myths undertaken by certain psychoanalytical movements; Marxist theory concerning myths as ideological projections of class structures, projections which act derivatively upon these structures in either a conserving or a revolutionary spirit—all these reflections and interpretations respond to questions which are somewhat differently put from the one with which I have been chiefly concerned. The same goes for the attempt at biologizing myth undertaken by Bergson, which sees in myth a functional equivalent of instinctual behavior replaced in the life of the human species by intelligence, and known especially in its perfect manifestations in the behavior of insects: the celebrated example of the praying mantis described in detail by Roger Caillois in analogy with various mythological motivations of primitive peoples. It is indisputable that in all areas of human culture mythologies have for centuries constituted an important form of communication and that there is hardly an area in culture where myth has not been employed as an instrument of organizing human communal existence.

However, in tracing the instrumental function of mythologies we have not automatically found answers to the question why various needs, in whose satisfaction mythologies have been active, have reached for just this instrument. The cultural inventiveness of myths ought to be understood prior to the understanding of a general reliance on its products in social conflicts, in integrational processes, and in the maintenance of the individual's spiritual homeostasis.

On the other hand, one may justly suspect that the assurance as such that the religious phenomenon constitutes a sui generis reality that cannot be decomposed into other categories, and is therefore (as was proclaimed by Otto and Scheler) indefinable is barren so long as we are unable to name the need whose intentional correlates are mythical objects. That is why it is worth explaining in what sense we may talk about the autonomous values of the mythological layer of social consciousness, and in what sense this autonomy is doubtful or puzzling, or permissible only as a mythological standpoint.

Now, it seems to me that such words as "autonomy" or "irreducibility" may have two sets of meanings with reference to mythical consciousness.

First, we may surmise that in this layer of culture, as in others, an emancipatory process comes to a head in which objects and behavior, which once had an instrumental sense, acquire an autotelic value not tied to their genealogy, although they continue to function in their instrumental roles as well. I say "we may surmise" since in fact we do not know the ultimate origins of mythology, just as we do not know the ultimate initial phase of any form of culture: of ritual, language, art, property, or law. Questions regarding the absolutely original cannot be posed in a form to which answers would take on the character of valid reconstructional hypotheses. So, as a rule, answers relate to remote analogies in other areas of culture or to the ontogenetic evolution; or assume—most often tacitly—a certain philosophical construct of human nature and on that basis recreate the initial phases of specific civilizational initiatives. While it is true that the philosophy of culture cannot avoid these questions, it is important that the philosophical assumptions necessary for the answers should be clearly realized and expressed.

The emancipation of mythical consciousness, understood as a developmental phase of culture, would in this sense consist in that the value ascribed to mythological symbols "turns irrational," that is, becomes something not requiring a justification in other needs unconnected with the mythical realm.

Such an interpretation concerns myth as an objectified element of culture but not myth as a content actually experienced. For it is unimaginable that myth in whatever phase, even in an unattainable *arché,* should be instrumentally experienced in the consciousnesses of its participants and at the same time perform whatever function connected with other needs of communal life. What is imaginable (although not provable) is that the effective functions of myth as a means of communication exhausted themselves, in their integrational and normative capabilities, and that only then was the perdurance of myth no longer dependent on its usefulness for these other tasks.

However, another understanding of that autonomy is acceptable, namely, one which does not assume any speculation regarding the temporal genealogy of myth but attempts to describe the character of needs intentionally referred to the mythological symbols. In that sense one can speculate that there are present in culture—without prejudice to the question whether eternally or only in a certain phase of civilization—such needs which cannot be satisfied without the participation of a mythological interpretation of the world. In such an attempt to understand myths the inquiry regarding its progressive emancipation may be suspended, and just such an attempt constitutes the content of our earlier reflections. We understand myth functionally in the sense that we refer its vitality to needs whose description as such does not assume myth as its source of satisfaction; but we do ascribe to it a value in itself to the extent that we proceed to establish that such satisfaction is unattainable without myth. In this sense, therefore, its autonomy depends on its being *irreplaceable in culture*. Needless to say, this does not include any assumption regarding the extracultural legitimacy of myth. On the other hand, interpretations which turn myths into an exchangeable instrument are unacceptable to the extent that they treat the replaceable functions of myths as exclusive. Equally, Cassirer's idea of seeing in myth an instrument which is specifically useful in moments of crisis or collective despair (at least under the conditions of contemporary civilization) seems wrong, unless he has in mind projective myths exclusively.

I have tried to present reasons for which the project of a total demythologizing of culture appears chimerical. An awareness of this situation is valuable to both sides: both in counteracting the destructive consequences of the natural rapaciousness of myth as well as in forestalling the dangers which arise from attempts— ineffective as they are—to suppress the mythical consciousness totally, since both dangers are constantly fermenting in cultures capable of growth.

Within the limits of philosophical meditation which makes culture its object, the sense of myth does not extend beyond the realm of culture, even when we accept the mythopoeic situations as a permanent element of human intercourse with nature or with other people. Within these limits, therefore, it is impossible to employ the term "autonomy" (or similar terms) with reference to mythical consciousness, if the meaning of that word were to suggest that the specificity of the mythical layer of culture is rooted in the specificity of its real sphere of reference. The validation of such a sense of the term "autonomy" is in itself a mythical project. A purely phenomenological constitution of a segregated sphere of myth, that is, its constitution as an intentional field, is of course possible. Such a procedure, if it is conceived as an eidetic cleansing of the myth phenomenon and comes about within the bounds of a transcendentally reduced consciousness, does admittedly bring the existential status of intentional objects in the mythical realm to the level of others; it does not, however, thereby endow them with reality, because a retreat from transcendental reduction is impossible without a cancellation of its results. In turn, the eidetic reduction itself, without a previous transcendental reduction is thinkable, but does not in any way prejudge the ontological status of its object, and leaves this matter as a separate question, independent of the results of the eidetic reflections.

If, finally, someone tries to describe a specific type of emotion correlated with mythical imaginings in a univocal coordination (for instance, Rudolph Otto's awe in the face of mystery), then, irrespective of the cogency of this description, the presence of this emotion does not take us beyond the realm of culture and psychology. This issue has not been the object of reflection in this study chiefly because of another usage of the term "myth" which covers areas beyond the specifically religious. In relation to myth thus conceived, Otto's idea is inapplicable. The consciousness of the world's indifference, deriving, as I attempted to show, from the very bifurcation of the human subject, cannot really be called an emotional phenomenon.

On the other hand, the proposed interpretation clearly does not accord with those which attempt to insert myth (in the narrower, that is, the religious sense) into human technological endeavors. Traditionalist evolutionist religious studies (Frazer's in particular) had detected in magic an ineffective (since based on false associations) system of attempts intended to force nature to perform required tasks; mythologically organized religion was supposed to be the next stage of these same endeavors: having persuaded themselves, after centuries of defeat, that nature is deaf to magical practices, human beings seemingly concluded that the regularities of the world are subject to control by forces higher than human and had transformed this observation into a system of mythological personifications, and at the same time had begun to propitiate with supplications and flattery those higher powers not responsive to spells and slow to obey. Religion is therefore a system of procedures which is opposed to myths on technical grounds but identical in its aim, which is to guarantee unenlightened communities the natural environment's sympathy. Both stages are concerned with practical results crucial in daily life, the second stage being the outcome of disillusion in the face of the ineffectiveness of techniques employed in the first stage. This second stage, religion, in turn inevitably reveals its own practical barrenness and gives way to scientific thinking which relies on precisely established rigors of testability of natural laws and slowly replaces primitive views regarding regularities in nature or the dependence of events upon the whims of supernatural beings.

This interpretation appears untenable chiefly because it makes inexplicable the persistence both of magical techniques and of mythological imaginings. Technological competences acquired by the method of trial and error establish themselves by way of normal conditioned reflexes, and the supposition that for thousands of years human beings were unable to correct a faulty conditioned reflex, that is, one based on a nonexistent connection, would have testified to a remarkable incompetence of their nervous system, unable to match the normal competences of any of the species endowed with a nervous system. Thus, the basic resistance both of magical practices and of mythological beliefs in the face of their practical ineffectiveness indicates that they resist, without a basic deformation of meaning, being included in the technological order of human behavior. Moreover, this kind of evolutionism does not explain why in fact at a certain moment people started interpreting the forces of nature as the revelation of teleologically acting beings; a technological orientation in no way imposes such an aberration. If, then, we bypass the speculative character of the presented chronology of magic-religion-science (for it is impossible not to admit that every theory which in general explains the birth of religious beliefs also rests on philosophical assumptions concerning human nature), one may assert that the consequences arising from this doctrine are probably susceptible to empirical falsification. As to the theory that all human behavior and products may be interpreted as actions or organs which increase the chances of biological survival, it is neither more nor less arbitrary than the doctrine which claims that human nature is codefined by an irremovable organ directed at mythological realities.

5

The perceptual reception of myth through its directly meaning-generating and normative content differs essentially from common perception which provides us with information about the world. This last is also subject to an evaluative selection (biologically designated) as regards criteria on a level of immediate perception. However, as the history of science demonstrates, we are capable of distinguishing the order of values from the order of information. This distinction has been absorbed in scientific and common-sense thinking to such a degree, the difference in epistemological status between that which informs and that which evaluates or commands has become so clear, that the description of perception whose specific quality is the nondifferentiation—in a single act—of both types of our reference to the world demands a certain effort. But this nondifferentiation is the peculiarity of mythical perception, which for that reason is a source of disorientation for every analysis which assumes that dichotomy between judging and valuing as most basically obvious. The normative content of mythical perception is not, in contrast to the valuation hidden in sense experience, directed by considerations of the possible exploitation of objects or of their role as sources of threat; this is an obligating and not a technological valuation. But the very word "valuation" is clumsy, since it suggests a separate act capable of being extracted as a separate order from the perceptual whole. In reality no such extraction occurs. In the reception of myth no distinction between that about which the myth speaks and that which it commands occurs. The legislating power of myth is contained in its direct perception—it is neither drawn out deductively nor superadded. The distinguishing in myth of information from commands, prohibitions, recommendations, and values is a derivative rationalization foreign to the perceived reality. We take up such rationalizations habitually in our reflections upon myth, schooled in this direction by many centuries of pressure of the intellectual rigors of science, but these rigors have created a deceptive obviousness which complicates our access to mythically organized consciousness where what myth entrusts to its participants is directly accessible in its contents and need not and even cannot be, without deformation, separately communicated or articulated as a conclusion or a moral. That is why it is difficult for us to comprehend the proper content of untranslatable expressions derivable from the mythical order which (like Tao) signify concurrently and indivisibly both primordial reality and the way of life for that person who has attained a view of that reality. The Gospel phrase, "I am the way, the truth, and the life," appears to an eye accustomed to rudimentary logical distinctions a jumble of words justified at best as metaphor translatable into several distinct utterances: "I am offering you proper directives," "I proclaim the truth," and "If you obey me I guarantee that you shall have eternal life," and so on. In fact, these sorts of conjectured metaphors are literal, do not demand to be understood and to be translated into the separate languages of values and information. One can participate in mythical experience only with the fullness of one's personality, in which the acquisition of information and the absorption of directives are inseparable. All names which participators in myths have given to their participation— "illumination" or "awakening" or such like—refer to the complete acts of entry into the mythical order; all distinctions of desire, understanding, and will in relation to these global acts is a derivative intellectual reconstruction. Also the concept of "faith" in the original sense of Christian mythology has precisely this meaning: the acceptance of myth in faith is not only contemporaneous but also identical with the act of trust in the presence of the divinity; it is the singular acceptance of myth in its fullness and the experience of "being accepted"; the subsequent distinction of faith as a variant in a state of intellectual conviction deforms the original content of the religious act. But this same homogeneity of the global act of acceptance or entry into the mythical order takes place in all those instances we have discussed and which do not belong to a specifically religious cultural stratum: we notice it equally in the normative power of the regulative principles of the intellect, in metaphysical and historiosophical constructions or in interpersonal relations. What we know and what obliges us is there everywhere embraced in the same act; everywhere there—in contrast to scientific thinking—the distinction between "is" and "ought to" is absent. But we then apply this distinction (brought to light by the filtering reflection) in such a way as though it were present in the original acts of participation. Hence the questions put to myths so often contain false assumptions. In asking whether myth serves to explain the world or is rather a defense against the destructive influence of intelligence upon practical skills, whether it is a classification of beings or rather a function of root emotions of fear, uncertainty, and despair—we force upon the mythical experience distinctions which are foreign to it. They are undoubtedly inevitable if the analytical work upon the mythological production of culture is to exist at all; they are, however, misleading if they are not constantly accompanied by the remembrance that a true participation in myth means a full act of a personal acceptance of mythical realities.

11

CONCLUSION

I have tried to explain why and in what sense our contributions to the human world, that is, the totality of the practical efforts of our brains, muscles, and hearts, are possessed of a meaning only thanks to the presence of the mythical layer of our existence. The passages through which this meaning-creating energy flows to all areas of our practical life appear at times blocked and incapacitated; however—and this too I have tried to record—such a stoppage cannot be total, since even the half-conscious and purely habitual skill in mythical interpretation is also hidden in the most common forms of our attitudes to the world, even when our life is filled with the desire to flee, with a willing self-deafening distraction and absorption in everyday events.

The irremovable share which mythological energy holds in everything which adds up to the specifically human *praxis*—technological, social, intellectual, artistic, and sexual—gives birth to the constantly reborn desire to have the content of mythical consciousness charmed into words which one could manipulate as freely as the ordinary reservoir of speech which organizes experience. We are unable to avoid these attempts; we are unable to give up the hope that our language, historically enslaved by the force of experience, can leap over them. Much, however, depends on whether we are able to distinguish the outcome of our onomaturgy from the language bound by the limits of experience. If we are not able, if therefore we ascribe the same manipulative (cognitive) value to words directed towards mythical reality as to words sprung from empirical material, we are condemned to barren disputes regarding the truth of conflicting myths—and all these disputes have as much intellectual dignity as the quarrels of Christian theologians regarding the proper formula for the Holy

Trinity or regarding the dogma of Transubstantiation. We must come to terms with the fact that expressions which attempt to record the intuitions of the mythical consciousness have a symbolic character which is sui generis; that they only seem to be amenable to argumentational confrontations.

The fear that in this area we are therefore condemned to total arbitrariness, that since there are no generally obligating criteria, everything is permitted and everything is equally justified, does not appear to be well founded. The mist of uncertain intuition, when it condenses in language, does not thereby acquire the value of a discovery; but we can—or we think we can—distinguish in mythical speech what is the deposit of a real concentration of feeling and imagination from what is a casual whim.

The same applies to religious myths of beginning, as well as to profane myths here described which measure various elements of experience against such unconditioned realities as "truth," "being," "value," and "humanity." It is characteristic of the first type of myth that it attempts to express what is universal in an unrepeatable singularity of a mythical occurrence. This circumstance, which Hölderlin had already attempted to grasp, means that the existential status of a mythical event is radically different from the status of factual experience; here fact is the carrier of universality and of a nontemporal message, preserving in itself the negation of its own facticity, that is, the negation of the world's contingency.

True, nonreligious mythical realities are not described in those pseudohistorical symbols and are not therefore chained to the singularity of an event. But from a functional point of view they are the same and reveal the labors of the same stratum of mind. They are an attempt in language to transcend the contingency of experience, the contingency of the world. They attempt to describe something that will give a noncontingent value to our perception and our practical contact with the world; they attempt to convey what cannot be literally conveyed, since our linguistic instruments are incapable of freeing themselves from the practical employment which summoned them to life. They therefore speak mainly through successive negations, doggedly and infinitely circling round the kernel of mythical intuition which cannot be reached with words. They are not subject to conversion into rationalized structures, nor can they be replaced by such structures.

This drive to nail with a word a reality of a categorically different existential status from the status of any components of practically usable experience, this unceasing effort to find a name for what is not contingent, gives the constitutive quality to human mythopoeic activities. From that point of view a difference between a religious and a nonreligious mythopoeic variant, although outstandingly significant for the history of culture, is of secondary importance.

Attempts at validating the mythopoeic activity within philosophy have normally been attempts to accommodate myths within a field reserved specifically for reason as a power radically different from common perceptual activities. Plato, Leibniz, and Husserl are the three most outstanding embodiments of this philosophical intention. All three attempted to reveal the contingency of the world to the extent that it is described from the standpoint imprisoned in the rigors of experience; all three also expected to overcome this contingency by purely philosophical means, summoning for this purpose separate cognitive powers which were to rise above the ordinary gift for abstraction and be identified as reasoning tools of Reason par excellence, as specifically human organs not traceable genetically to animal skills. The illusoriness of all these attempts consists in the hope that this search for a noncontingent resting point for thought can be validated as an achievement of discursive reason. Devoid of this hope to a large extent, the philosophy of our time aims rather at recognizing discursive reason as an extension of ordinary perception, giving up the attempt to validate philosophically the products of the mythopoeic layer of existence and confining itself to an effort of defining the boundaries of the permissible tasks of ordinary perception and reason. The mythopoeic energy cannot be converted. The efforts to record its activity will not cease; it is however essential to avoid a mystification in which this effort is granted the dignity of reason explaining the world of experience—assuming the word "explain" maintains the same common usage as in the proposition "Lightning is explained as an electrical discharge," and suchlike.

But even the greatest scrupulousness in distinguishing between the mythologico-symbolic and the technologico-cognitive functions of consciousness will not result in a permanent removal of clashes between their activities. Contrary to Durkheim's speculation, participation in myth is not just a superstructure of spiritual life, necessary for an effective transmission of authority and norms and completing harmoniously the technological activities of the community. Participation in myth is—at least in our culture—an eternal challenge to reason, an usurpation in relation to the monopoly of power which the needs of our bodies "encountered in nature" maintain over us. The split of consciousness is a split of life into orders which cannot maintain a mutual attitude of totally isolated regions through indifference nor of sympathetically complementary cooperators combining in the construction of the totality of existence. The animal order and the mythical order are turned against each other in unfriendly mistrust and (at times) hostility—at least in a culture whose own mobility does not permit a state of equilibrium. We have no cause to believe in a final synthesis which would demonstrate the illusoriness of this conflict, its temporality. We have no cause to be deceived either by a historic or a cosmic eschatology, promising us the ultimate fulfillment of history and an irreversible conciliation of all energies active in culture—in a word, the growth of the temporal world into a triumphal harmony of point Omega (to use the Teilhardian expression). For a participant in myth the mutations of the human world may, of course, be understood as the growth and ripening of a divinity in the body of the cosmos or as stage-by-stage progress of man's empirical existence to a place in which this existence is identified with human destiny. However, a philosophy of culture which observes the clashes between mythological longing and the pressure of empirical, biological existence must be wary of such hopes; it will note the areas of chronic struggles and will rather be revealing situations in which the very fragility of our existence appears in mythical consciousness as a sign of decline, while a mythological overcoming of that fragility appears to the eyes of rational and technologically directed consciousness as a sickness of culture. The empirical consciousness will remind us as Jehovah reminded Ezekiel: "Will you say to those who will come to kill you, 'I am God'—since in the hands of your assassins you are man and not God?" On the other hand, the mythical consciousness will repeat, as Jesus did on the mountain, that it is impossible to serve two masters and that we should not concern ourselves for our bodies. We may, it is true, imagine a state of institutional truce in the relationship between the mythological and the rationalized orders of culture; we may even imagine a mutual neutralization from a purely logical point of view of both orders. Finally, we may conclude that some individuals are capable, in the psychological sense, of maintaining these orders in harmony or an appearance of harmony. However, as repositories of values active within our culture, the orders are unsuitable for a synthesis, although we are forced to move within each, although therefore, willy-nilly, we have to serve two masters. No rational argument will present binding reasons which will command us to judge one or the other of these orders unequivocally as a shadow masking that other "true" reality; none will allow us to decide which of the two orders—the mythical or the phenomenal—makes up the real world and which arose in imagination; in which of them we are awake and which forms part of our dreams; which is the face of the world and which its mask. Between the point of view for which the realities of experience constitute the only "hard" existence, while everything else arises from the miasmas of the imagination, and the one for which, conversely, authentic reality lies "on the other side," while the impermanent world of phenomena must appear a flickering of an unimportant surface— between these two points of view it is impossible to decide by reference to reasons regarded on both sides as valid. This is because for each of the conflicting parties the validity as such of the reasons given by the opponent already assumes criteria of valuation rooted in the opponent's arbitrary decision. For a worshiper of mythical realities proofs brought against myths matter little, since the validity as such of the proof is grounded on an exclusive trust in practical values applicable in the empirical world. An opponent will in turn be claiming, with equal right, that mythical reasons, if they are to be valid, require a previous agreement to mythical convictions. The futility of this clash would not in the end be so burdensome were it not that both points of view, incapable of synthesis and eternally in conflict, are after all present in everyone of us, although in varying degrees of vitality. They have to coexist and yet they cannot coexist.

This coexistence, both inevitable and impossible, should not however cause us to lament or to be a pretext for indolent and desperate reflections upon the degeneracy of human fates. On the contrary, cultural momentum always has its source in a conflict of values from which each side attempts, at the expense of the other, to claim exclusivity, but is forced under pressure to restrict its aspirations. In other words, culture thrives both on a desire for ultimate synthesis between these two conflicting elements and on being organically unable to ensure that synthesis. The achievement of synthesis would mean death to culture, just as much as an abandonment of the will to synthesis would be. The uncertainty of the projects and the impermanence of the conquests turn out to be a condition of a creative survival of culture. The story of culture is an epic splendid through its fragility.

INDEX OF NAMES